MUSICIANS INSTITUTE

ESSENTIAL CONCEPTS

EAR TRAINING

For the Contemporary Musician

by Keith Wyatt, Carl Schroeder and Joe Elliott

ISBN 0-7935-8193-1

HAL•LEONARD® CORPORATION

7777 W. BLUEMOUND RD. P.O. BOX 13819 MILWAUKEE, WI 53213

Visit Hal Leonard Online at
www.halleonard.com

In Australia Contact:
Hal Leonard Australia Pty. Ltd.
4 Lentara Court
Cheltenham, Victoria, 3192 Australia
Email: ausadmin@halleonard.com

Contents

Getting Started

Every musician has heard about or met someone who seems to be able to pull music right out of the air and play it without effort—someone who can hear a tune once and then play it from memory, dream up a melody and write it down without ever checking a single note, or play fresh, inspired solos night after night. These musicians are able to imagine, interpret, and play musical patterns without any apparent lag between thought and execution. Though this ability is often referred to as a "gift"—that is, something bestowed upon a person by an outside force—it rests on concrete skills that can, in fact, be learned. The skill that ties together all of a musician's resources—technique, intelligence, and creativity—is **ear training**, and it is the key to becoming not just good but great.

Here are a few frequently asked questions about ear training, along with answers, to help you get started properly:

Do I have to be born with great ears?

No. Talent may be defined as the ability to effectively link imagination to execution without a great deal of effort. Just as it's true that, for example, some people naturally shoot a basketball better than others, it's also true that some musicians naturally play their instruments better than others. But it is also true that just as average basketball players can develop outstanding skills through dedicated physical training, average musicians can develop outstanding skills through dedicated ear training. After years of experience working with thousands of musicians at all skill levels, the authors can verify that while talent undoubtedly provides a head start in ear training, in the end it is far outweighed by such factors as motivation and discipline.

Do I have to know music theory?

No. Music is a form of language, and like any language, it includes a vocabulary and certain rules for usage. The bigger your vocabulary and the better you understand how to use it, the more freedom you have to express yourself. We will explain the rules of harmony, melody, and rhythm as necessary in order to help you understand how sounds are organized, but the emphasis is on practical application, not theory (however, as noted below, you do need to know what musical notation means).

If you want more complete explanations of theory and notation, we recommend that you obtain a popular- or jazz-based theory text (classical theory uses very different terminology and systems of organization). In particular, we recommend *Harmony & Theory: a Comprehensive Source for All Musicians* by Keith Wyatt and Carl Schroeder (MI Press/Hal Leonard Corporation), which uses the same terms and concepts as this book.

What do I need to know to get started?

This method is designed to be an introduction to ear training, but we do need to make a few basic assumptions about your skill level:

1. **You can hear pitch differences.**
    If you honestly can't tell whether a given note is higher or lower in pitch than another note, you'll need to work with a private teacher who can give you specific guidance on how to develop this skill before you begin this method.
2. **You have some basic skills on either a guitar or a keyboard.**
    You don't need any special amount of technique, but you do need to have some way to play and visualize melodies and chords on an instrument. At a minimum, what you need to be able to do is:
    *   Find notes on your instrument by alphabet name (C, D, E, etc.)
    *   Play major and minor triads in different keys
    *   Play the major scale in different keys

If you've just started playing and can't yet do these things, work with a method book or take a few lessons before starting this book. It won't take long to learn the basics, and your ear training will progress much more quickly.

3. **You understand basic musical notation.**
   You do *not* need to be a sightreader (i.e., someone who can read musical notation in tempo), but you *do* need to understand what various notes and rhythms mean. Any fundamental theory or technique book will explain musical notation.

4. **You have regular access to your instrument and a CD player.**
   A CD player with easy-to-use pause, cue, and review functions is essential for gaining maximum benefits from the CDs that accompany this book.

5. **You have regular time to practice in a quiet, private place.**
   Set up a practice station where you keep your instrument, CD player (with either speakers or headphones), manuscript paper, blank paper, pencil, eraser, and a clock or watch all ready to go. The less you have to do to get ready each time you sit down to practice, the easier it will be for you to stay disciplined.

How do I practice?

Each exercise in this book includes specific practice instructions. There are exercises that develop your singing, listening, writing, visualizing, and playing skills, sometimes individually and sometimes all at once. The CD examples that accompany the text are designed to improve specific skills, and they provide you with a step-by-step method that combines each new element with those previously learned.

How often do I need to practice?

Ear training is best accomplished through short, focused practice sessions of 15-30 minutes every day rather than longer, infrequent sessions. You cannot "cram" ear training the same way you might study for a test. Like learning a new language, you have to hear it and use it regularly over a period of time before it begins to sink in. When you practice, if you find yourself getting tired, take a break—when you are tired, your ability to hear patterns will suffer. Do something else for a while and then come back to ear training when you are fresh.

How do I use the CDs?

The CDs that accompany this book include dozens of exercises containing hundreds of individual examples. In most cases, the text explains the first example in detail, and then you complete the rest of the examples using the same demonstrated method. Within each exercise, examples are arranged progressively, beginning with easier material and gradually becoming more difficult. (The demonstration example is designed to be moderately difficult in order to prepare you for all levels within the exercise.)

These exercises were *not* designed to be performed in "real time"; that is, you are expected to pause during and between examples while you sing, analyze, visualize, write, and/or play. You should also expect to repeat individual examples, perhaps many times, before you move on to the next exercise (that's why you need a CD player that allows you to move back and forth in small increments).

What if I want more exercises?

Although the CD exercises provide a considerable amount of practice material, in some cases you may want more. The time-honored way to get this is *do it yourself*. If you want more practice on major scale melodies, for example, write some examples for yourself, record them, put the recording away for a day or two, then test yourself with it. Better yet, trade recordings with a friend. As you record your own exercises, you'll have the added benefit of learning the patterns much more effectively than when you only hear someone else play them.

Do I need to start at the beginning?

Depending on your prior experience, you may be able to skip over parts of this book, or you may be challenged from the first page. This method is progressive, but your background may not be—if you've never studied ear training in an organized way, you are likely to have holes in your understanding and abilities. It is worth your while to start at the beginning in order to fill in gaps that could later undermine your progress. On the other hand, don't waste time and energy going over topics you already understand well—move quickly until you reach a level that challenges you.

How fast should I move through the book?

There is no simple answer to this question—it's a matter of several factors including how much experience you have and how often and how effectively you practice. Just as with physical training, ear training requires discipline and repetition, and you won't always move forward at a constant pace. Some topics may be relatively easy for you to master, while others take more time. There is no overall time limit on any of the exercises, but avoid staying on one exercise for too long—the resulting frustration could cause more harm than good. Rather than striving for perfection on each exercise as you go, work until you are accurate about 8 out of 10 times. After you listen to an exercise for long enough, you will begin to memorize it, and that's good—it means the sounds are becoming part of your vocabulary, and it also means that you should move on.

How do I know if I'm getting better?

Ear training is a process, not an event. Training your ears is like lifting weights—for a long time nothing seems to be happening, then one day you look in the mirror and are surprised to see how much you've changed. Ear training progress may seem slow in coming, but after you've begun to build a solid foundation, one day you will find yourself listening to a piece of music and understanding the patterns without much effort—proof that you are getting better whether you're aware of it or not.

How far will this book take me?

The focus of this book is on training your ears to understand the patterns of contemporary popular music, i.e., music that is beat-driven and organized around common systems of melody and harmony, which includes most rock, R&B, blues, country, pop, and their multiple subcategories. Jazz- or classically-oriented methods will take you farther into complex sounds, but the skills taught in this method support further development in any style you like.

Part I
Major Tonality

The simplest definition of music is "organized sound"; thus, to understand how music works, you need to understand some of the rules by which melodies, harmonies, and rhythms are organized. First among these is the major scale—the source of the melodies, chords, and chord progressions that together make up the most widely used system of sounds in popular music, **major tonality**.

Pitch and Tonality

1

The first step in training your ears is to develop your ability to **match pitch**; that is, to accurately match with your voice a note played by an instrument.

Matching Notes within Your Vocal Range

Matching pitch is like tuning an instrument—when the two notes match, they stop vibrating against each other and sound "smooth," in much the same way that adjusting a camera lens brings an image into sharp focus. If you have never consciously matched pitch before, you may find yourself doing so without giving it much thought. On the other hand, you may have difficulty knowing if you are singing in tune or if you're even close to the note you are trying to match. If this is the case, start singing well below or above the pitch and slide your voice up or down until you hear the two notes synchronize.

EXERCISE 1

Play middle C on your instrument, and match it with your voice (sing "ah"), sliding up or down as needed until the notes are in tune. Play the note again. This time listen, match it mentally *before* you sing it, and then sing it precisely, without sliding up or down into the pitch. Repeat the exercise, matching other notes within your vocal range. If it takes you longer than a few seconds to match a note, practice matching different pitches on your instrument at least 5-10 minutes a day until you can match them quickly and correctly (for now, avoid notes that are higher or lower than you can sing comfortably).

Every great musician has the ability to **pre-hear** notes; in other words, they have learned to accurately predict what a note on their instrument will sound like *before* they play it (see "Perfect Pitch vs. Relative Pitch" below). This is the skill that allows composers to write without using an instrument and improvisers to create melodies spontaneously while they perform. Matching notes in your head before singing them is an essential pre-hearing exercise that will help prepare you for higher levels of ear training.

Perfect Pitch vs. Relative Pitch

Perfect pitch, the ability to identify the name of a given note without comparing it to a known pitch, is a trait that some people seem to possess from birth. A person with perfect pitch can, for example, tell you the name of any random note played on an instrument or name the key of a piece of music by seemingly "pulling it out of the air." Clearly, this is a handy musical tool to have, but is it essential to becoming a good musician? The answer is "no"—in fact, relatively few outstanding musicians have perfect pitch, and conversely, those who do possess it are not necessarily outstanding musicians. Instead, most musicians train themselves to use **relative pitch**, that is, to quickly and accurately identify musical patterns in relation to a known pitch. Some ear training methods are designed to develop perfect pitch, but most, including this one, develop relative pitch. In the end, the practical result—the ability to understand musical patterns by ear—is the same.

Chapter 1

Matching Notes Outside Your Vocal Range

Most instruments have a range that extends beyond the limits of the human voice, so once you can match pitch confidently within your vocal range, the next step is to learn to match notes above or below your range.

What is your vocal range? You can determine your vocal range by matching pitch with a piano or guitar, going from the lowest note you can sing precisely and consistently to the highest. This can change somewhat over time depending on several factors including your vocal skill, time of day, humidity, fatigue, and overall health. A head cold can seriously affect your ability to find and hold pitch, so test your range when you're clear-headed, and don't strain your voice.

Matching pitch outside your range is possible because notes that are double or half the frequency of a given note—called **octaves**—sound virtually "the same" although the actual pitches are obviously higher or lower. For example, any white key on the piano has the same letter name as the eighth white key above or below it (octave literally means "group of eight").

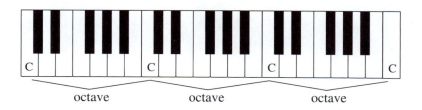

As a result, you can match any pitch no matter how high or low it is by finding the equivalent note in an octave within your range.

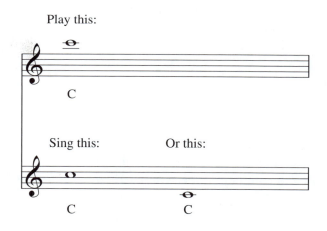

EXERCISE 2

Play a note on your instrument that is within your vocal range, match it directly, then keep singing it while you play the same note in a higher or lower octave. Next, play a note that is considerably above or below your range and match it within your range. Go back and forth until you can quickly match notes outside your range with notes inside your range.

Tonality

Different styles of popular music—rock, R&B, jazz, new age, country, rap, metal, and so on—differ radically in terms of instrumentation, textures, chords, melodies, and grooves, but all popular musical styles share one fundamental characteristic—they are all **tonal**. This means that each piece of music is based around a single, fundamental tone, or **tonic**. The tonic is often described as sounding like "home"; it's the note around which all of the melodic and harmonic patterns are organized. You certainly don't have to be a musician to recognize tonality—after all, you cannot hum a melody without it. What separates musicians from ordinary listeners, though, is how we use this concept as a basis for understanding the musical relationships that hold a piece of music together.

EXERCISE 3

Without accompaniment, sing "Happy Birthday." Which note in the melody is the tonic?

If you chose the first note, the highest note, or the lowest note of "Happy Birthday" as the tonic, think again. It's the *last note.* Sing the first and last notes of "Happy Birthday" back to back, and notice how the last note feels more like "home"; in musical terms, the melody **resolves**. Even in the rare cases where a melody does not contain the tonic, melodic patterns revolve around the tonic as planets revolve around the sun—tonality is an invisible, binding musical force that, like gravity, keeps everything from flying off in different directions.

As you'll see in the coming chapters, once you have found the tonic of a piece of music, it's possible to identify every other note in the melody and harmony by comparing it to that single note (which is often simply called "**one**").

EXERCISE 4

Spin the dial on the radio and listen to tunes of different styles, each time locating "one." Often the tonic will be more prominent in the bass line than in the melody. Sing "one" and hold the note, while you listen to how the chords and melody move around within the tonality.

The Major Scale

2

After the ability to match pitch, the most important basic ear training skill is the ability to sing and identify notes of the **major scale**.

Describing Sounds with Numbers

In the language of popular music, sounds are described with numbers, beginning with "one" (the tonic). Just as inches or centimeters describe the physical distance of one object from another, musical numbers describe the distance of notes from the tonic, and the major scale provides the equivalent of a ruler. The notes of the major scale are numbered from **1** to **8**, with the tonic assigned the number 1 and the other scale tones ascending in order up to the octave, which is number 8. The pattern then repeats, so "8" becomes the "1" of the next higher octave of the scale.

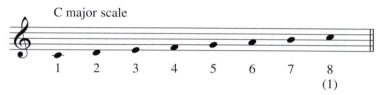

After basic pitch matching, the next step in training your ear is to learn the major scale pattern and identify each note by number. Again, your voice provides the best tool.

Singing Major Scales

Singing the major scale is a form of pitch matching, but instead of matching one note you're matching a whole pattern of notes. Fortunately, this pattern is so ingrained in our musical surroundings that it's intuitive, but singing it with a high degree of accuracy and consistency may take some practice. Follow these steps to make sure you stay on pitch.

EXERCISE 1

1. On your instrument, pick a tonic that is comfortably within the lower part of your vocal range (C is usually a good choice), and play the major scale up to the octave.

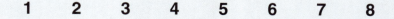

        C   D   E   F   G   A   B   C

2. Play the scale again, this time singing the scale step number of each note while carefully matching pitch with your instrument (you don't need to sing the letter names, only the numbers).

        1   2   3   4   5   6   7   8

3. When you can accurately sing the scale while matching pitch with your instrument, sing the scale again by numbers without accompaniment. Play the octave to confirm that you stayed on pitch all the way through. It is very important not to let your voice drift away from the scale pattern—match pitch with your instrument until you're consistently accurate.

Depending on the pitch of the tonic, the notes of the scale may ascend out of your vocal range. If this happens, drop these upper notes into a lower octave as described in Chapter 1 ("Matching Notes Outside Your Vocal Range"), and continue singing the scale in the lower octave, like this:

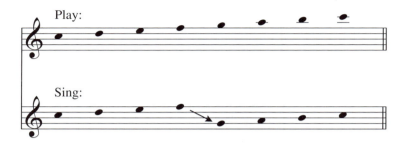

Changing octaves in the middle of a scale may be tricky at first, but it's also a good exercise that tests both your ability to match pitch and your knowledge of the scale pattern.

EXERCISE 2

Sing major scales from random tonics, matching pitch with your instrument at the tonic and octave as described above. Repeat the exercise as needed until your pitch is consistently accurate from any note.

Descending Major Scales

Melodies move down just as often as up, so the ability to sing major scales descending is equally important. Descending major scale tones are numbered backwards, from 8 to 1.

EXERCISE 3

Pick a tonic note that's comfortably within your upper vocal range, and sing a descending major scale while playing along on your instrument.

8   7   6   5   4   3   2   1

Follow the steps outlined for singing ascending scales. If the scale moves down out of your vocal range, sing the step at the bottom of your range an octave higher, then complete the scale from there. Continue singing descending major scales from random pitches. Repeat the exercise as needed until your pitch is consistently accurate.

3 Major Melodies

The pattern of notes that makes up the major scale is the same no matter what pitch is used as the tonic, so relationships based on scale step numbers are independent of any particular key. Understanding the relationship between numbers and scales is the best way to develop a reliable sense of relative pitch.

Converting Numbers to Melodies

Just as the notes of the major scale can be described with numbers, numbers can be converted to pitches and used to create major scale melodies.

EXERCISE 1

1. Pick any random note on your instrument as a tonic ("1"), and sing a one-octave ascending major scale, using a number for each scale step.
2. From the same tonic, sing the following numbers in order, matching each scale step number with the appropriate pitch:

$$1 \quad 2 \quad 3 \quad 2 \quad 1$$

3. Play the same melodic pattern on your instrument and compare the results.
4. Sing the same melody from a different tonic. Although the pitches are different, the pattern itself is identical in relation to the tonic.

The musical term for moving a melody to a new key is **transposing**. Using numbers, it's relatively easy to transpose melodies since the relationship between the tonic and the rest of the major scale is the same regardless of key.

EXERCISE 2

Using the same method, sing the following sets of numbers in at least two different randomly chosen keys:

1	2	3	2	3		
1	2	3	4	3		
1	2	3	4	5		
1	2	3	4	5	6	5
1	2	3	2	3	4	5

EXERCISE 3

Use the same method on a descending scale, starting the melodies on the octave (8) rather than the tonic (1):

8	7	6	7	8		
8	7	6	7	6		
8	7	6	5	6		
8	7	6	5	4	5	
8	7	6	5	6	7	8

Turning Melodies into Numbers

Melodies can be identified and written down, or **transcribed**, by converting the notes into numbers. Since the pattern of the major scale is the same in every key, using the number system means you can transcribe major scale melodies even if you don't know the name of the key or the key signature—you just have to know where "one" is and how to sing the major scale with exact pitch. When you hear the melody, you match it to the major scale and number the notes appropriately.

The next exercise demonstrates this method using pre-recorded examples. Once you know the method, it will work even when the melodies become longer and more complex.

CD1 Track 1

EXERCISE 4

1. Listen to **CD1**, **Track 1**. The first note you hear (before the exercise itself) is the tonic (C). Match pitch with the tonic, then pause the CD and sing the major scale ascending and descending from that note in order to "tune" your ear.
2. Start with Example 1. Listen to the example, and count the number of pitches in the melody. On a blank piece of paper, draw a short line for each note, like this:

    ____   ____   ____   ____   ____

3. Listen to the example again, and sing along until you have it memorized. Wherever you hear the tonic, write "1" in the appropriate space. You do not have to transcribe the notes in order from first to last. If you recognize the third note before you know what the second note is, that's OK—every note you know will help you find the notes you don't know:

    _1_   ____   _1_   ____   ____

4. Notice the contour or shape of the melody. The melody starts on the tonic, goes up in pitch, then back to the tonic, then up again. Each time it ascends in pitch, how far does it go? Write down the scale step numbers:

    _1_   _2_   _1_   _2_   _3_

5. Play the melody on your instrument to check the accuracy of the pitches. (Remember, the tonic is C.)
6. Repeat the same process with the rest of the examples on Track 1. The exercise includes melodies with anywhere from three to six notes. The "answers" are included in the Answer Key found in the last section of this book. Do the whole exercise before you check your work. If any particular exercise gives you trouble, go back to it, but do not repeat the ones you get right. If you want more exercises of this type, record them yourself as described in "Getting Started."

Melodic Skips

4

The notes in a melody move in two ways: 1) by **step**, that is, up or down the scale in consecutive order, or 2) by **skip**, passing over one or more scale steps. All melodies include skips, and some skips are nearly as common as steps.

EXERCISE 1

1. Pick any comfortable note as a tonic, and sing a major scale up to the octave and back, to tune your ear.

2. Sing the following melody (the major scale up to the fifth step and back):

   1   2   3   4   5   4   3   2   1

3. Sing the same melody from the same tonic, but sing the bold tones out loud and the others silently:

   1   2   **3**   4   **5**   4   **3**   2   **1**

4. Eliminate all but the bold notes. The melody is now *all* skips:

   1——3——5——3——1

EXERCISE 2

1. Sing the following ascending sequence of interval skips from any comfortable tonic until you reach the octave:

   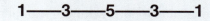

   1——3   2——4   3——5   4——6   5——7   6——8

2. Sing the same sequence in reverse, from the octave to the tonic:

   8——6   7——5   6——4   5——3   4——2   3——1

EXERCISE 3

Sing each of the following melodies from any comfortable tonic. If you have a hard time singing the skips accurately, sing the major scale step in between as you did in Exercise 1, then sing the skip again without the extra step. With some experience, it will become easier to make the skips directly.

1	2	3	5	
1	3	4	5	
1	3	5	6	5
1	3	5	4	5
1	3	2	4	5
8	7	6	5	3
8	6	5	6	8
8	6	5	7	8
8	6	5	4	3
8	6	5	3	1

Notating Melodies Outside the Octave

Most popular vocal melodies tend to fall into a narrow range—about an octave and a half at the most. Within these limits, melodies often extend below the tonic, above the octave, or both. When using the numbering method to identify scale steps, we need to have some means of indicating when a melody extends above or below a single octave.

Scale steps below the tonic
When melodies include scale steps that extend below the tonic, notate the numbers by underlining. For example, sing the following melody, using any note as the tonic. The 7 is underlined, indicating that it is one step <u>below</u> 1, not seven steps above it:

1   2   3   2   1   <u>7</u>   1

Scale steps above the octave
To show notes that extend above the octave, keep counting up from 8; that is, use 9 (an octave higher than 2), 10 (an octave higher than 3), etc:

1   3   5   7   8   9   10   9   8

NOTE: This type of notation for pitches outside the octave is *not* standard musical notation—it is designed specifically for the purpose of completing the exercises in this book. Later, we'll replace this numbering system with traditional music notation.

Chapter 4

Pitch Freezing

The next exercise concentrates on melodies containing skips. As you listen to more complex melodies, at some point you may find yourself losing track of "1" or losing your place in the major scale pattern. If this happens, use a technique called **pitch freezing**:

1. Go back to the beginning of the melody, locate "1," hit "pause" on your CD player and hum it.
2. While still humming "1," hit "play" and let the melody move forward to the note where you first began to lose your place.
3. Immediately hit "pause" again and match pitch with the "unknown tone." Sing back and forth between "1" and the unknown tone, counting the major scale steps until you match the scale step number of the note.

Use the same technique whenever you hear a note that you can't identify—find "1," freeze it, find the unknown tone, freeze it, and compare the two.

The goal of ear training is to learn to hear and identify not just individual notes, but whole phrases, just the way you hear music when you listen for pleasure. Using the pitch freezing method to break melodies down to individual notes is a very technical way to analyze music, but it's a necessary foundation for developing accuracy and speed. As you begin to recognize longer phrases, eventually you won't need to stop and analyze the notes as often. You'll get back to hearing music as music again, but this time with a trained ear.

CD1 Track 2

EXERCISE 4

CD1, **Track 2** contains melodies with skips (including below the tonic and above octave). Transcribe each example using the following method:

1. Listen to the melody, and sing it.

2. Locate the "ones." (In this illustration, the blanks indicate the as-yet-unidentified notes.)

1   ____   ____   ____   1

3. Identify the remaining notes, using the pitch freezing method as needed. Indicate the note below the tonic with an underline.

1   3   2   <u>7</u>   1

Remember: you don't have to identify the notes in order. Start with the notes you're completely sure of, and then use those to help identify the rest.

Intervals

5

he steps and skips that make up melodies are, in the language of music, commonly called intervals. An **interval** is the distance between any two notes. Intervals are named according to the number of scale steps they contain. For example, the distance from the tonic to the second note of the major scale, containing two scale steps, is called a **second** interval (or simply a "second"). The distance from 1 to 3, containing three scale steps (1, 2, and 3), is called a **third**.

Intervals measure the distance between notes no matter where they occur in the scale. For example, 1-3, 3-5, and 6-8 are all third intervals because they all contain three scale steps. Also, intervals are measured the same way both descending and ascending—the distance from 3-1 is the same as from 1-3; both are thirds.

The exercises in Chapter 3 were all stepwise, while those in Chapter 4 included intervals of a third. The exercises in this chapter introduce the next most common melodic intervals: fourths, fifths, and sixths.

Fourths and Fifths

Fourths contain four scale steps, and **fifths** contain five.

EXERCISE 1

1. Pick any comfortable note as a tonic and sing an ascending, one-octave major scale to tune your ear.
2. Sing the following melody with the bold notes out loud and the others sung silently:

1   2   3   4   5   6   7   8

3. Repeat the melody, singing only the bold notes:

1   3   5—8

The leap from **5** to **8** contains four scale steps, making it a fourth interval.

4. Repeat the exercise with the following melody, beginning on the octave:

8   7   6   5   4   3   2   1

5. Sing only the bold notes:

8   7   6   5—1

The leap from **5** to **1** contains five scale steps, making it a fifth interval.

Chapter 5

EXERCISE 2

Sing each of the following melodies from any comfortable tonic. Each contains thirds, fourths, fifths, or a combination. If you have a hard time singing the skips accurately, sing the scale steps in between as you did in Exercise 1, identify the interval, and then sing it again without the extra steps.

1	2	3	5	8
1	5	4	5	8
8	7	6	5	1
8	5	4	3	1
8	7	6	5	8
8	5	3	5	1
1	5	6	5	8
1	5	3	5	8

Sixths

Sixths, containing six scale steps, are the next most common melodic intervals.

EXERCISE 3

1. Pick any comfortable note as a tonic and sing the following melody with the bold notes out loud and the others sung silently:

    1   **2**   **3**   4   5   6   7   **8**

2. Repeat the melody, singing only the bold notes:

    1   **2**   **3——8**

    The skip from **3** up to **8** contains six scale steps, making it a sixth interval.

3. Repeat the exercise with the following melody (note that the melody extends below the tonic):

    1   2   **3**   2   1   <u>7</u>   <u>6</u>   **<u>5</u>**   1

4. Singing only the bold notes:

    1——3——<u>5</u>——1

    The interval from **3** <u>down</u> to **5** contains six scale steps, making it, too, a sixth interval.

CD1 Track 3

EXERCISE 4

CD1, Track 3 contains melodies that begin on the tonic (or octave) and include third, fourth, fifth, and sixth intervals. Transcribe the melodies using numbers. If a melody goes below the tonic, underline the note, and if it goes above the octave, use a higher number as described in Chapter 4.

Remember to use the pitch freezing method as needed—if you can't identify a note or interval, locate "1" (or any other note that you *can* identify) and count the scale steps in between.

Starting on Notes Other Than the Tonic

Up to this point, you have focused exclusively on melodies that begin, and in most cases end, on the tonic or octave. In practice, it is at least as common for melodies to start on other scale degrees.

EXERCISE 5

Pick any note as a tonic, and then sing the following melody with the first four notes soft and the rest loud:

(1   2   3   4)   **5   6   5   4   3   4   5**

Even though the tonic is not one of the bold notes, the relationship between the bold scale tones maintains a strong sense of tonality; "1" is felt even if it is not heard. (You may recognize this melody as "London Bridge Is Falling Down"—proof that melodies starting on notes other than the tonic are not necessarily more complex.)

It may take some practice before you can quickly identify melodies that don't begin or end on the tonic. In "real" music, where the melody develops over a period of time and other instruments provide accompaniment, the tonality is usually easy to identify. If the melody begins on a different note, sing the tonic, sing the starting note of the melody, and count the steps between them to figure out what scale step the melody begins on.

EXERCISE 6

Sing each of the following melodies, picking a comfortable note as the tonic and locating the starting note by singing the proper interval (avoid using the scale steps in between). Play the melodies on your instrument to check for accuracy only *after* you've sung them on your own.

5	6	5	3	1
5	1	7	2	1
5	8	5	6	5
3	2	1	3	5
3	4	5	3	1
3	5	6	5	1

EXERCISE 7

Transcribe the melodies on **CD1, Track 4**. These melodies all start on notes other than the tonic. Before each example, the tonic (C) will be played. If necessary, count the scale steps in between the tonic and the starting note to determine what scale step the melody begins on.

Practicing Away from Your Instrument

One of the goals of ear training is to develop your ability to recognize musical relationships without using your instrument, and a very effective way to do this is to apply the number-note relationship to your everyday life. Any set of numbers you run across—phone numbers, addresses, license plates, etc.—can be turned into a melody, and because they're random they stretch your ears more than deliberately "musical" examples.

EXERCISE 8

Pick any comfortable note as a tonic and sing this imaginary telephone number as a melody:

876-5321

Except for the single third interval skip between 5 and 3, it's a stepwise descending major scale. Of course, most random telephone numbers are not as melodic as this, but by using this idea, you can literally "sing the phone book." You can also include the numbers 9 and 0 in the melody—just as "8" is the octave of "1," "9" is the octave of "2," and "0" is the octave of "3."

EXERCISE 9

Sing the following telephone number:

890-9858

If the note you pick as the tonic makes the rest of the melody too low or too high for your vocal range, pick a different tonic. Since the notes have the same relationship regardless of the key you choose, any key that's good for your voice will do.

EXERCISE 10

During your normal daily activities, find at least five sets of numbers—phone numbers, license plates, a driver's license or ID number, etc.—and sing them using this method. By learning to practice away from your instrument or CD player, you will be able to train your ear nearly any time and any place.

Remember: singing is the single most important thing you can do to improve your ear. Once you are able to match pitch and sing the major scale accurately, you have the basic tools that will enable you to identify any musical pattern you hear.

Meter and Rhythm

6

The fundamental method behind relative pitch ear training is to make comparisons between unknown, unfamiliar melodies and familiar, unchanging patterns such as the major scale. The same idea holds true for rhythms. Rhythmic combinations occur within a framework of **meter**, and once the sound and feel of a given meter become familiar, that meter is the pattern to which rhythms can be compared.

Meter

Meter is a pattern of accented (strong) and unaccented (weak) beats in a repetitive pattern. The most common metric patterns contain two, three, or four beats. Every style of music is built around a certain type of meter (or "feel"), for example:

Two-beat meter
Based on the left/right foot pattern of the march, two-beat meter is common to the folk music styles of many European countries (polka, Irish/Scottish, Italian, etc.) and their American descendants, including traditional country music and rockabilly.

STRONG - weak

Three-beat meter
The more common name for three-beat meter is the *waltz*, a dance style originating in Europe that includes variations such as Viennese waltz, country waltz, and jazz waltz.

STRONG - weak - weak

Four-beat meter
Nearly every contemporary popular musical style, including rock, funk, R&B, hip-hop, blues, and jazz is based on four-beat meter.

STRONG - weak - weak - weak

Time Signature

The meter of a piece of music is indicated by the **time signature**. The time signature contains two numbers, one above the other. The upper number indicates how many beats are in the pattern, usually 2, 3, or (most often) 4. The lower number indicates what note value receives one beat—2 for a half note, 8 for an eighth note, or 4 for a quarter note. Since four-beat meter with the quarter note as the basic note value is the most common feel in popular music, the most common time signature is 4/4:

4	=	number of beats in a measure
4	=	note value of each beat

This time signature is so common, in fact, that it is also known as "common time" (or "c"). In light of its predominance in contemporary popular music—which is the focus of this book—all of the rhythm exercises will be based on that time signature.

EXERCISE 1

Listen to the radio, and tap your foot to the first piece of music you hear. How many beats form the basic rhythmic pattern, or meter? If you're listening to a popular music station, chances are the answer will be four. (In most styles, the drummer clearly defines four-beat meter by hitting the snare drum on the second and fourth beats, a pattern called the **backbeat**.)

To find examples of two-beat or three-beat meter, you may have to find a country or jazz station. The only time you are likely to hear meters such as 5 or 7 (commonly called "odd" meters) will be on jazz or more adventurous rock stations.

Rhythms

Just as beats are combined to form meter, they are divided to form **rhythms**. Rhythms are notated using notes and rests of various duration:

| whole note | half note | quarter note | eighth note | sixteenth note |

| whole rest | half rest | quarter rest | eighth rest | sixteenth rest |

Combinations of quarter notes and eighth notes (and their corresponding rests) make up the largest number of rhythms found in popular melodies and chord patterns, so they are what we'll focus on initially.

To identify and transcribe rhythms, you first need a systematic method for counting beats. In 4/4 meter, for example, the beats are numbered 1-4:

Each quarter note can be divided into two eighth notes (♪ ♪). Eighth notes occurring on the beats are called **downbeats**, and eighth notes occurring between the beats are called **upbeats**. Downbeats and upbeats correspond to the tapping motion of your foot when counting the meter; that is, downbeats occur when the foot strikes the floor, and upbeats occur when the foot is in the air.

The location of any eighth note in a bar can be described by the number of the beat and whether the note is on a downbeat or an upbeat—for example, a note may occur on "the downbeat of 2" or "the upbeat of 3." Upbeats are also described verbally by the word "and," which is notated by the symbols "**&**" or "**+**" (using this terminology, the *upbeat* of 3, for example, is also called "the *and* of 3").

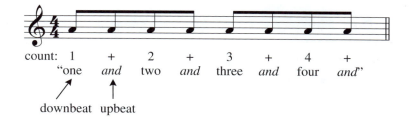

Two-Beat Phrases

Like a spoken language, rhythms are made up of short phrases that combine to make longer ones. The shortest practical eighth-note rhythmic phrases are two beats in length. Since there are a limited number of these phrases, once you've learned them, longer phrases will be much easier to recognize.

Attack and Sustain

Every rhythm can be measured in two ways: **attack** and **sustain**. Attack refers to the point in the bar where the rhythm "hits," and sustain refers to how long the note lasts. For example, a quarter note hitting on a given beat is sustained twice as long as an eighth note hitting on the same beat—the attacks are the same, but the sustains are different.

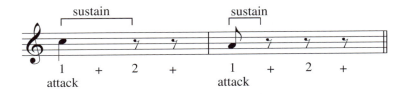

In terms of fundamental ear training skills, it is much more important to identify the attack than it is to calculate sustain. As long as the attacks are in the right places and the total number of notes and rests in a bar match the time signature, different note values may be considered equivalent.

Using only eighth notes and eighth rests, there are fourteen possible rhythmic combinations within two beats (not counting all notes or all rests):

In addition to memorizing the various combinations of eighth notes and rests, you also need to develop a consistent method for transcribing rhythms.

EXERCISE 2

Listen to **CD1**, **Track 5**, and follow this method for transcribing each two-beat eighth-note rhythm (use a pencil, and have an eraser handy):

1. Above the staff, make a small mark for each possible eighth note or rest (in a two-beat phrase, there are four possible eighth notes):

2. Tap your foot in time with the beat (quarter notes), listen to the example, and sing along, using the accented syllable "*dah*" to match the notes and "*tuh*" to mark the empty eighth notes. Memorize the phrase quickly, then sing it back to yourself while using the **dot-tap method**: Tap your finger in steady eighths, and whenever you hear a note, place a dot on the staff beneath the point where it occurs:

3. Once you know where each note occurs, write the note and rest values on the staff and erase the other marks:

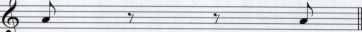

As with melodies, the goal of rhythmic ear training is to learn to recognize complete musical phrases, not just the small, technical ingredients that make up a rhythm. At first, it's necessary to break phrases down into small, unmusical pieces in order to understand their structure, and then rebuild them. The "dot-tap" method is a very effective way of breaking rhythms into their smallest parts because it has the added advantage of being physical. By actively singing, tapping, and marking the page in time with the rhythm, you're reinforcing the information on several levels and making it feel more musical. With some experience, you will be able to hear rhythms as whole, musical phrases.

Four-Beat Phrases

When two, two-beat eighth-note phrases are combined, the resulting phrase is four beats in length, or one bar of 4/4 meter. All of the same methods you used for transcribing two-beat phrases still apply, but the combined, short phrases form longer phrases that have a distinct sound of their own. As phrases become longer, it is critical that you maintain the proper number of beats in each bar—in a bar of 4/4, there can be no more and no less than eight eighth notes or rests (or their equivalent in larger note values).

EXERCISE 3

CD1, **Track 6** contains examples of four-beat phrases in 4/4 meter. Transcribe each example using the dot-tap method developed in Exercise 2 above.

Again, attack is more important than duration; when you compare your answers to the Answer Key, as long as you maintain the proper number of beats in the bar and notate the attacks in the proper places, you may differ in how you notate the length of the notes without being wrong.

Two-Bar Phrases

Rhythmic phrases longer than one bar conform to all of the same rules and methods as shorter phrases. The exact number of beats in each bar must be strictly maintained in accordance with the time signature. Now that you have gained some experience with rhythm, it's time to look more closely at the length (sustain) of each note as well as the attack. Longer notes clearly sound different than shorter notes, and you need to learn some methods for notating different note lengths. Aside from eighth, quarter, half, and whole note and rest values, there are two other common ways that longer notes can be notated: dots and ties.

Dots and Ties

A small **dot** placed to the right of a note head or rest has the effect of increasing its length by half. Most common of these is the dotted quarter note (or rest), which is the equivalent in length of a quarter plus an eighth, combined into one sustained note value.

dotted quarter note

Another way of notating a sustained note is by using a **tie**, a curved line connecting two notes of smaller value. Ties are used when a rhythm is sustained past the number of beats allowed in a single bar, in effect crossing the bar line. The two tied notes sound the same as a single, longer note value, but tying prevents the problem of violating the time signature by having too many or too few beats in a bar.

In the example above, the last note of measure 1 is one and one-half beats long; without using a tie, measure 1 would be a half-beat too long and measure 2 would be a half-beat too short. Splitting the note and tying it across the bar line sounds identical but maintains the proper number of beats in each bar.

Ties are also commonly used when a note is sustained across the middle of a measure. In the following figure, the second example sounds identical to the first, but the two-beat phrase on the left is kept visually distinct from the two-beat phrase on the right.

this phrase: *is more clearly notated like this:*

CD1 Track 7

EXERCISE 4

CD1, Track 7 contains two-bar rhythmic examples for transcription. Use the dot-tap method, and make sure each measure contains the correct number of beats.

Once you've transcribed the examples, compare your answers to those in the Answer Key, which are written using standard notation including dots and ties. Again, correctly locating the attack of each note is more important than precisely notating the sustain, but in the end both factors are significant in making the music look the way it sounds.

7 Transcribing Melody and Rhythm

After working with major scale melodies and eighth-note rhythms separately, the next step is to transcribe musical phrases by putting the pitches on the staff, in rhythm. At the same time, you can begin to develop the ability to connect your ears, hands, and instrument using the technique known as **visualization**—that is, picturing how your fingers will play a phrase before you actually play it. Transcription and visualization are both essential parts of the complete ear training cycle.

Understanding Musical Notation

In order to use standard musical notation, it's essential that you understand three things:

1. Rhythmic values and how to notate them
2. The names of notes on the staff
3. How the major scale is built (i.e., key signatures)

For the purposes of learning how to notate, we'll simplify things for now:

1. All melodies will be written in the treble clef.
2. All melodies will be in the key of C major (no sharps or flats).

When you have some experience transcribing melodies and rhythms within these boundaries, you'll find it much easier to make the transition to other keys and to the bass clef. No matter what key or range the melody is written in, the relationships of notes to the tonic (i.e., relative pitches) are the same; only the details of notation are different.

Here, for your reference, are the notes of a C major scale, as written on the staff in treble clef:

A **note about concert pitch:** Concert pitch is the international reference for instrument tuning, designated as A=440 cycles per second. With this reference point, instruments anywhere in the world can be tuned to precisely the same pitch, so any two pianists reading the note middle C, for example, will produce "C's" with identical frequencies. For this reason, pianos and other instruments designed around the same pitch are called "concert" or "C" instruments. Some instruments, however, are designed so that a player reading middle C will produce a different pitch; these are called **transposing instruments**. Guitar and bass are two examples of transposing instruments—when a player of either instrument reads middle C, the sound they produce is an octave *below* that of a piano. This raises a question: When you transcribe keyboards, guitar, and bass, which octave should you write the notes in? There are two answers. First, follow the rules of each instrument—for guitar, middle C on the staff corresponds to the fifth string, third fret, and for bass, it's first string, fifth fret (each of these notes sounds an octave below the piano's middle C). Match pitch between your instrument and the melody, and write in the appropriate octave. The second answer is, any octave will do. Our goal is to develop your sense of relative pitch, and since the relationships between the notes are the same regardless of octave, write the melodies wherever you're most comfortable for now, and worry about the details of transposition later.

EXERCISE 1

CD1, **Track 8** contains major scale melodies with eighth-note rhythms. Transcribe each example using the following method:

1. Use staff paper, a pencil (*not* a pen), and have an eraser handy. Write the clef and time signature (4/4) on the staff:

2. Listen to the example, and, using the "dot-tap" method, lightly pencil in the rhythm of the notes below the staff. Double-check the rhythms against the example to confirm their accuracy.

3. Listen to the melody, match pitch, and identify the scale step numbers of the notes. (Before each example, you'll hear the tonic played separately.) Write the numbers above the staff opposite each rhythm. Again, double-check for accuracy:

4. Convert the scale step numbers to notes on the staff, beginning with dots placed in the proper position for each pitch. Since these examples are all completely within the C major scale, no accidentals (i.e., sharps or flats) will be needed.

5. Add the proper rhythmic notation to the notes on the staff, and erase the rhythmic sketch below the staff. The example is now complete. Play it on your instrument, and match it against the original example to confirm the accuracy of the notes and rhythms:

As you become a more experienced transcriber, you'll be able to write notes and rhythms directly on the staff as you hear them. Transcribing in musical notation is like learning a new alphabet—it takes time and practice to learn the symbols and write legibly. Reading music is a very good way to improve your notation and transcribing skills, since it teaches you how proper notation should look.

Chapter 7

Visualization

The ability to **visualize** how a phrase will look and feel when it is played on an instrument is an invaluable part of ear training, especially for performing musicians. When you properly visualize a phrase, i.e., picture your fingers playing it in your mind's eye, you can work out the fingering and other technical problems before you ever touch your instrument. Visualization is a skill that all experienced improvisers, composers, and sightreaders develop to a high degree.

EXERCISE 2

You can begin to practice visualization with one simple exercise: sing along with yourself as you play, connecting the sound of the notes, the physical shape of the passage, and the sound of your voice. Don't worry about the quality of your singing voice—it's the physical sensation of singing and breathing that counts, not the precise pitch or tone. This is not an exercise that you do for a certain number of minutes a day; it's a habit that you form by doing it *whenever* you play.

EXERCISE 3

Another good visualization exercise is to sing or hum a short phrase, visualize how your fingers will look while playing it, and then play it on your instrument. This develops the skill of pre-hearing (see Chapter 1)—that is, predicting the sound and feel of a phrase before you play it. If your imagination is running ahead of your playing ability, this is an excellent way to close the gap.

Visualization improves your sense of melody and phrasing along with your technique, keeping your ear and physical skills in balance. Visualization is not really a separate exercise, it's part of every exercise—integrate it into your playing right away until it becomes a natural reflex, and eventually you will gain the ability to practice and write music away from your instrument.

CD1 Track 1-4,8

EXERCISE 4

Review **CD1**, **Tracks 1-4** and **8**. Sing each example, convert it to scale step numbers, visualize it, and then play it. As you move forward through this book, make visualization a routine intermediate step between listening, singing, and playing.

Sightsinging

8

Ear training has been a part of every musician's development since instruments were first invented, and the process took a great leap forward about a thousand years ago with the development of musical notation and **sightsinging**—the skill of singing music directly from the printed page. After centuries of musical evolution, sightsinging remains one of the fundamental tools of ear training.

A Step-by-Step Approach

Sightsinging combines some by-now familiar skills:

- Recognizing rhythmic phrases
- Matching pitch
- Singing major scale melodies including steps and skips

Here is a typical major scale melody followed by the step-by-step method for singing it:

Step 1: Rhythm

Taking the same approach that you used for transcribing, work with rhythm and pitch separately. First sing the rhythm alone:

Step 2: Pitch

Now look at the pitches without the rhythm.

Chapter 8

What's the key? (In this example, it's C major—no sharps or flats.) Does the melody start on the tonic or a different scale tone? Beneath each pitch, write the scale step number. Each line and space represents a single scale step, and the key signature provides all of the necessary sharps or flats.

Now that you've numbered each pitch, you're ready to sing:

- If you have an instrument—guitar, bass, or keyboard—play the tonic, and match it with your voice.
- If you do not have an instrument, you can pick any note that lies comfortably within your vocal range and call it "1." Whether or not it is truly the correct pitch doesn't matter at the moment, since the entire melody can be sung by relative pitch regardless of the actual key.

Once you have a tonic, sing the major scale up and down to "tune" your ear, then sing the pitches using any syllable ("la" is fine). Cover up the numbers, and sing the notes alone. With a little practice, you will recognize the visual patterns formed by stepwise melodies and standard interval skips. In musical notation, the sense of "up" and "down" and the visual distance between notes is designed to reflect the sound of the music.

Step 3: Combine rhythm and pitch

After you've explored the pitches and rhythms separately, put them back together and sing the complete melody. Start slowly and work your way up to a reasonable tempo—having laid the groundwork, this should happen quickly.

Check the example by playing it on your instrument to see if it matches what you sang. (If you were singing by relative pitch, it might be in a different key.)

As you do more sightsinging, you won't find it necessary to go through all of these individual steps. Just as you've learned to read English by instantly recognizing groups of letters as words and groups of words as phrases, you can learn to instantly recognize combinations of notes and rhythms as complete musical sounds.

A note about solfeggio: Solfeggio is the "do-re-mi" system of singing musical pitches, and it has long formed the foundation of traditional sightsinging methods. A major advantage of solfeggio is that it is unique and specific—the syllable "do," for example, represents the tonic and nothing else—whereas numbers have multiple meanings that can sometimes be confusing. However, relatively few popular musicians (at least in the United States) are trained in solfeggio, and the language of popular music relies heavily on numbers to describe musical relationships. We will use the number system throughout this book, but any readers who are already trained in solfeggio are encouraged to continue using that system if it helps them progress more quickly.

EXERCISE 1

Sightsing the following examples (treble clef, 4/4, key of C major):

If these examples sound familiar, they should—they're the same melodies you transcribed in the previous chapter. Any of the other melodic examples in this book can also be used as sightsinging material. The principles of sightsinging are the same regardless of the style or complexity of the music—written music is everywhere, and with the basic skills you've learned in this chapter plus some experience, you can eventually sightsing any of it. A good source of beginning sightsinging material can also be found in the basic method book for any instrument, since beginning exercises are designed to be easy to read. Whenever you look at a piece of written music, make it a habit to sightsing and visualize before you play it, and you'll find that when you do play, the results will be much more musical.

Interval Quality

9

Intervals can be measured in two ways. The first is by the number of scale steps the interval contains—its quantity (second, third, fourth, fifth, etc.). Quantity provides a general measurement of distance, but intervals sharing the same quantity don't always sound alike. To tell them apart, you need another, more exact measurement—this is the interval's **quality.**

Major vs. Minor Seconds

Here are the notes of the C major scale:

C   D   E F   G   A   B C

Notice how the letter names are laid out on the page—E and F are closer together than the other letters; so are B and C. This is not a mistake. If you look at how the scale is built on a guitar, bass, or keyboard, you'll see that those pairs of notes are on adjacent frets or keys, while all of the others are separated by one fret or key. Although the distance between any two adjacent scale steps—C to D, or E to F, for example—is a second interval, clearly not all second intervals are alike. C to D is the distance of a **whole step** (two frets or keys apart), while E to F is the distance of a **half step** (one fret or key apart). Each has a distinct sound.

To identify the exact size of an interval, we need to specify its *quality.* Quantity and quality combine to make up the complete name of an interval. The distance from C to D is not just a "second interval"; it is a **major second.** The distance from E to F is a **minor second.** Again, the names are the same whether an interval is ascending (E-F) or descending (F-E). Measuring interval quality is like using a ruler—the distance between any two given objects is the same whether you start measuring from one or the other.

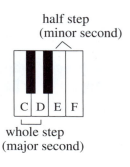

half step
(minor second)

whole step
(major second)

EXERCISE 1

1. From any comfortable tonic, sing the first two notes of an ascending major scale. The distance from the tonic up to the second degree is a major second (or whole step).
2. From the same tonic, sing the first two notes of a descending major scale. The distance from the tonic down to the seventh is a minor second (or half step).
3. From the same tonic, sing a *minor* second ascending and a *major* second descending (use a syllable like "la")—this will probably be tricky at first, and you may have to check your accuracy on your instrument.
4. Sing major and minor seconds ascending and descending from other notes at random.

Once you can sing these intervals exactly, you'll find it much easier to identify them when you transcribe. Plus, since all diatonic (i.e., seven-note) scales are built from a series of whole steps and half steps, the ability to accurately sing major and minor second intervals is a skill that enables you to identify *any* note—if it isn't in the scale, it can be no more than a half step away. To apply this ability effectively, you need to become both accurate and quick, which takes practice, but the basic skill is surprisingly simple.

EXERCISE 2

CD1, Track 9 contains major and minor second intervals for identification. Listen to each one, sing it, and then identify it.

Other Interval Qualities

The complete names of all intervals include both quantity and quality. Complete interval names of the major scale steps (as measured from the tonic) are as follows:

scale step	interval quality
second	**major** second
third	**major** third
fourth	**perfect*** fourth
fifth	**perfect*** fifth
sixth	**major** sixth
seventh	**major** seventh
eighth	**perfect*** octave

*The term "perfect" will be explained in Chapter 10.

Notice that these intervals are all either major or perfect. All other interval qualities can be described in relation to major scale steps as follows:

- Any major interval lowered by a half step becomes **minor**.
- Any minor or perfect interval lowered by a half step becomes **diminished**.
- Any major or perfect interval raised by a half step becomes **augmented**.

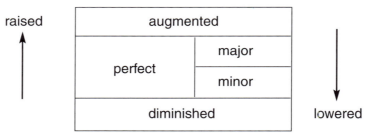

The following list illustrates the common interval names that result from raising or lowering major scale tones by a half step (some interval names exist in theory but not in everyday practice—only the common intervals are included here):

lowered ←	major scale interval →	raised
minor second	major second	augmented second
minor third	major third	
	perfect fourth	augmented fourth
diminished fifth	perfect fifth	augmented fifth
minor sixth	major sixth	
minor seventh	major seventh	
	perfect octave	

The first step in becoming familiar with different interval qualities is to sing the major scale with half step alterations.

EXERCISE 3

1. From any comfortable tonic, sing up to the second degree of the major scale (use "la").
2. From the major second, sing down a half step to the minor second.
3. Sing the tonic again, and sing the minor second without the major second in between.
4. Sing the tonic, the major second, then up a half step to the augmented second.
5. Sing the tonic, and sing the augmented second without the major second in between.

Repeat the same exercise from each scale tone, singing up or down in half steps to find all of the common intervals.

After you've familiarized yourself with the sounds of the various intervals as they relate to the major scale, we'll then learn the most common uses of intervals within melodies.

Melodic Intervals

10

Hearing intervals within the framework of familiar melodies is the best way to lay the foundation for hearing them as independent sounds. In theory, any two notes can make up a **melodic interval**, but in practice, certain intervals are far more common than others.

Thirds

Third intervals come in two qualities, major and minor. The **major third** (abbreviated "ma3") contains two whole steps, and the **minor third** (abbreviated "mi3") contains one whole step and one half step. In the major scale, the major third is heard frequently as the melodic interval between the tonic and the third scale degree.

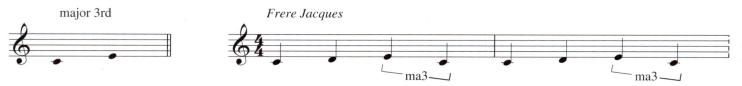

Sing the melody above (it's the familiar French nursery rhyme "Frere Jacques"). Notice that it goes up three scale steps and then returns to tonic in a single skip—the fact that the interval is descending rather than ascending does not affect either its quantity or quality. In melodies, intervals go up and down with approximately the same frequency.

Another very familiar melody features a minor third interval, which is found between the third and fifth degrees of the major scale. This is the interval between the first two notes of the nursery rhyme "Rock-a-Bye Baby" as well as Brahms' "Lullaby":

These two intervals are very often used in combination, as at the beginning of "The Star Spangled Banner," for example:

As you become familiar with the sound of these intervals, you will begin to recognize them within any number of melodies. While they occur frequently in the major scale context just described, intervals are also common in other settings, so it's also important to learn them as individual sounds apart from a particular scale.

EXERCISE 1

On your instrument, play a note that's at the center of your vocal range, and match pitch. Sing a major third interval ascending (use "la"), then go back to the same note and sing a minor third interval ascending. Including the starting note, major thirds encompass five frets or five keys (including black keys), and minor thirds encompass four frets or four keys. After you sing, play the intervals to check whether you sang them accurately.

Next, sing major and minor thirds *descending* from the same note. This might be more difficult, because the same melodic interval sounds quite different depending on whether it's ascending or descending. Unconsciously, your brain tends to identify the first note as "1," which makes some descending intervals sound as if they go outside the major scale. Learning specific melodic references where the interval is used in context is one of the best ways to overcome this reflex—for example, a helpful reference for the descending major third is Beethoven's "Fifth Symphony," which begins with the famous *dat-dat-dat-daaaaah*. Perhaps even more familiar is "Three Blind Mice," which begins with a descending major scale (3–2–1); the first and third notes are a descending major third interval apart. (See Exercise 8 in this chapter for more about song references.)

Choose another note and repeat the exercise. Each time you do it, visualize the interval on your instrument, and then play it to see if you visualized it correctly. Repeat this exercise until you can sing major and minor thirds quickly and accurately in both directions from any note you choose.

CD1 Track 10

EXERCISE 2

CD1, **Track 10** contains major and minor third intervals for identification. Listen to each one, sing it, and then identify it. If you want more intervals to practice, you can make your own version of this exercise—record a large number (20-30) of major and minor thirds played from random notes on your instrument, set the recording aside for a day, then play it back and test yourself.

Fourths and Fifths

The fourth and fifth degrees of the major scale are **perfect** in quality, as in "perfect fourth" and "perfect fifth." The term "perfect" was originally chosen to reflect the feelings these intervals evoke; in contrast to the emotional qualities of happiness or sadness conveyed by major and minor third intervals, perfect intervals are emotionally neutral, like a blank, white canvas.

Perfect fifths in major scale melodies occur most often between the tonic and fifth degree, while perfect fourths are most often found between the fifth and the octave (both intervals are featured strongly in the main theme from the film *Star Wars*, for one example).

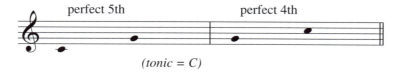

(tonic = C)

Because of their similar qualities and the fact that they both have a strong tendency to resolve to the tonic, perfect fifths and fourths are easily confused with one another. Counting scale steps is one way to tell them apart; another is to practice singing them back-to-back.

EXERCISE 3

Pick any comfortable tonic, sing up the scale to the fifth degree and then sing the interval from 1-5 without the scale. Continue up the scale from the fifth degree to the octave and then sing the interval from 5-8 without the scale. Reverse the process, singing from the octave to the fifth scale degree, then from the fifth degree to the tonic.

NOTE: The terms "fifth" and "fourth" can have two meanings, one referring to a specific scale degree and the other to the interval *between* scale degrees—it's important not to confuse them.

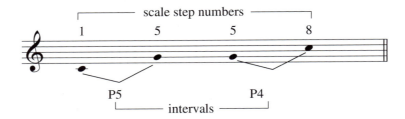

EXERCISE 4

Pick a note and sing a perfect fifth interval ascending; return to the note, then sing a perfect fourth interval ascending. Next, sing a descending fourth and a descending fifth consecutively from the same note. When singing fifth intervals, the lower of the two notes generally feels like the tonic (as in the interval 5-1), while in fourth intervals it's the *higher* of the two notes that feels like the tonic (as in the interval 5-8).

CD1 Track 11

EXERCISE 5

CD1, Track 11 contains a mixture of perfect fourth and perfect fifth intervals for daily transcription practice. If you need more practice, make your own recording as described previously.

Sixths

Sixth interval qualities are either major or minor, as in "major sixth" and "minor sixth." In its typical major scale setting, the **major sixth** is found between the perfect fifth scale degree and the major third scale degree above it:

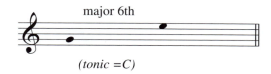

(tonic =C)

This is the interval between the first two notes in the folk song "My Bonnie Lies Over the Ocean" as well as in traditional three-bell door chimes.

The **minor sixth** interval is commonly heard between the major third degree of the scale and the octave (an interval prominent in the Scott Joplin ragtime melody "The Entertainer," well-known as the theme from the motion picture *The Sting*):

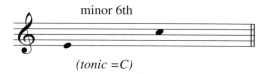

(tonic =C)

EXERCISE 6

As you have done with thirds, fourths, and fifths, sing major and minor sixths ascending and descending from various tones.

CD1 Track 12

EXERCISE 7

CD1, **Track 12** contains major and minor sixth intervals, ascending and descending, for melodic interval identification practice.

To help you remember the sound of each of the various intervals, the traditional method is to relate it to a familiar song that highlights it—for example, the major sixth ascending is the first two notes of "My Bonnie," etc. Of course, if you do not know these particular songs, they won't help you, so the best approach is to create your own list of references that you know well. It may take a while to come up with melodies that feature all of the intervals, but you don't have to be limited to any particular style or even to vocal melodies—a favorite guitar lick, for example, might be the best way for you to remember a certain interval.

EXERCISE 8

Fill in your own melodic interval song references next to the list of standard references shown here:

standard reference   your reference

Minor 3rd

ascending: Brahms' "Lullaby"
              "Rock-A-Bye-Baby"
              "Smoke On the Water"   _____

descending: "Hey Jude"
              "The Star Spangled Banner"   _____

Major 3rd

ascending: "Frere Jacques"
              "When the Saints Go Marching In" _____

descending: Beethoven's *Fifth Symphony*
              "Three Blind Mice"   _____

Perfect 4th

ascending: "Here Comes the Bride"
              "Amazing Grace"
              "La Cucaracha"   _____

descending: Theme from *Born Free*   _____

Perfect 5th

ascending: "Twinkle, Twinkle Little Star"
              Theme from *Star Wars*   _____

descending: Theme from *The Flintstones*
              "Feelings"   _____

Minor 6th

ascending: "The Entertainer" (theme from *The Sting*)
              Theme from *Love Story*   _____

descending: Theme from *Love Story*   _____

Major 6th

ascending: "My Bonnie Lies Over the Ocean"
              Doorbell chime/NBC theme
              "Soul Man" guitar intro   _____

descending: "Nobody Knows the Trouble I've Seen"
              "Take the A Train"   _____

Harmonic Intervals

11

Melody and rhythm are two fundamental ingredients of music; another is **harmony**. Harmony is the sound of two or more notes occurring at the same time, and the simplest form of harmony is the interval. Harmonic intervals contain the same notes and have the same names as melodic intervals, the only difference being that the notes occur *together* rather than separately. In theory, any two notes can form a harmonic interval, but in practice certain intervals are far more common than others, and these include thirds, fourths, fifths, and sixths.

Thirds

Like their melodic counterparts, harmonic thirds come in two qualities, major and minor.

While all of the ingredients of melodic and harmonic intervals are identical, the fact that both notes of a harmonic interval are heard simultaneously adds an extra step to the identification process.

EXERCISE 1

On a guitar or piano, simultaneously play both C and the E above it (a major third). If the two notes are played with equal force, the E will nonetheless tend to sound louder, clearer, and more prominent than the C—as a rule, the ear perceives higher pitches more clearly than lower pitches. Match pitch with the E, then slide your voice down until you match pitch with the C. Sing the two notes again, this time ascending from C to E to form a familiar melodic major third.

Repeat the exercise with C and E♭, a minor third. In each case, the extra step in identifying harmonic intervals is to separate the pitches from each other and convert them to a melodic interval. It is generally easiest to match pitch with the higher-pitched note first and then the lower note.

CD1 Track 13

EXERCISE 2

CD1, Track 13 contains major and minor harmonic third intervals for identification. Listen to each interval, match pitch with the higher and lower notes, convert them to an ascending melodic interval, and identify it.

Fourths and Fifths

Perfect fourths and fifths are often used together to form one of the most common chord types in rock music: the **power chord.** Power chords consist of a root, the note a perfect fifth above, and often the octave, which is a perfect fourth above that. The name "power chord" reflects the strong, clear quality of these perfect intervals.

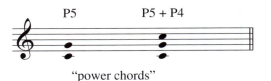

"power chords"

The method for identifying harmonic fourth and fifth intervals is the same as the method used for third intervals—sing the notes separately and identify them as you would melodic intervals.

EXERCISE 3

Play C together with the G above it. Match pitch with the G, slide your voice down until you match with the C, then sing the two notes as an ascending melodic interval. Do the same thing with C and the F above it. Since the two intervals are identical in quality but not in quantity (the number of scale steps), another means of telling them apart is to match pitch with each note of the interval and then count the major scale steps in-between.

CD1 Track 14

EXERCISE 4

CD1, Track 14 includes fourth and fifth harmonic intervals for identification practice.

Sixths

The process of identifying harmonic sixth intervals is again the same—separate the notes and identify them as melodic intervals.

Chapter 11

EXERCISE 5

Simultaneously play C and the A above it. Match pitch with A, then with C. Repeat the process with C and A♭. It can be tricky to tell these two interval qualities apart when they're played from random notes, but recalling the "door chime" sound of the major sixth can help clarify the difference: Sing the two notes of the interval (C-A) with the imaginary "1" (F) in between, and if it matches the door chime, it's major; if it doesn't sound quite right, then the interval is probably minor.

CD1 Track 15

EXERCISE 6

CD1, **Track 15** includes harmonic major and minor sixth intervals for transcription.

Inversions

Any pair of intervals that combine to form an octave are called **inversions**. These pairs include the major third and minor sixth, minor third and major sixth, and perfect fifth and perfect fourth.

Inversions are easily confused with one another because, in spite of their different quantities (and qualities), each contains characteristics of its partner. This is especially true when they are played as harmonic intervals, so the only sure way to avoid confusing an interval with its inversion is to carefully match pitch and count steps. With practice, you will be able to hear harmonic intervals as single sounds and identify them without first converting them into melodic intervals, but even experienced musicians still occasionally use this method to double-check their first impressions.

Major and Minor Triads

12

A harmonic interval—two notes played together—is the smallest unit of harmony. It takes two or more notes played simultaneously to form a **chord**. Most basic chords are built by stacking notes in intervals of a third, and the simplest of those are called **triads**. Triads are chords that contain three different notes, or chord tones, played at once:

root: the fundamental note of the triad
third: a major or minor third interval above the root
fifth: a perfect, diminished, or augmented fifth interval above the root

Like intervals, triads are described according to their quality. Four common qualities result from the different combinations of thirds and fifths, with the two most-used qualities being **major** and **minor**. We'll explore the other two triads—augmented and diminished—in later chapters.

Major Triads

Major triads contain a **root**, **major third**, and **perfect fifth** (these tones may be repeated in more than one octave or arranged in various orders, but triads by definition contain three *different* chord tones):

The first step in learning to identify any triad quality is to be able to correctly sing the **arpeggio** of the triad, that is, the chord tones one at a time.

EXERCISE 1

From any given pitch, sing the first five notes of a major scale ascending and descending:

1   2   3   4   5   4   3   2   1

Next, sing only the first, third, and fifth notes ascending and descending:

1   3   5   3   1

Finally, add the octave, singing the root, third, fifth, and octave ascending and descending:

1   3   5   8   5   3   1

Continue this exercise from other pitches. Your goal is to learn to sing major triad arpeggios quickly *without* singing the scale tones between.

Chapter 12

Minor Triads

Minor triads are constructed of a **root**, **minor third**, and **perfect fifth**.

EXERCISE 2

From any comfortable pitch, sing the note a minor third interval above, return to the root, and then sing the note a perfect fifth interval above:

1   ♭3   1   5

Sing these three notes ascending and descending in order:

1   ♭3   5   ♭3   1

Add the octave and sing all four tones ascending and descending:

1   ♭3   5   8   5   ♭3   1

Continue this exercise from other pitches.

EXERCISE 3

Pick a note and sing major and minor arpeggios back-to-back; repeat from other notes at random.

Identifying Major and Minor

It is accurate to say that major triads sound "happy" and minor triads sound "sad" when heard as individual sounds, but when heard in chord progressions these simple distinctions become much less dependable. To be certain of a triad's quality, you need to know how to analyze the structure by ear.

CD1 Track 16

EXERCISE 4

CD1, Track 16 contains assorted major and minor triads for you to identify. Analyze the structure of each one using the following method:

1. Listen to the example, and match pitch with the root (in these examples, the root is always the lowest note).
2. Play the example again, and sing up in steps until you match the third, then sing the melodic interval between the root and third.
3. Finally, identify this interval. For major and minor triads, the quality of the third determines the quality of the triad, so you can ignore the fifth for now.

The most important part of this method is to let your ear guide you to the correct quality by matching pitch *before* you decide what it is; otherwise, you'll be merely guessing. If you have even the most basic pitch-matching skills, your voice will intuitively match the sound of the third. The critical next step is to name the quality correctly. If you find this difficult, review Chapters 10 ("Melodic Intervals") and 11 ("Harmonic Intervals") and continue working with CD1, Tracks 10 and 13 (melodic and harmonic thirds).

Triad Progressions

13

Just as the major scale is a source of melodies, it can also be a source of chord progressions. Progressions that are made up of major and minor triads built from the notes of a single major scale are called **diatonic harmony**.

The Harmonized Major Scale

If you harmonize each note of a major scale with the third and fifth scale steps above it, the result is a series of triads—some major and some minor (plus one other quality, the diminished triad, which we'll discuss shortly). These represent the triads available within the key—in other words, the diatonic harmony.

mi = minor, ° = diminished; all others are major

Just as the major scale is built from a specific pattern of whole steps and half steps, diatonic harmony consists of specific pattern of triad qualities, and this pattern is exactly the same in all major keys; that is, the first chord is *always* major, the second chord is *always* minor, and so on, regardless of the tonic. Like scale steps, the chords can be numbered—allowing us to speak of them in relative terms. But whereas scale steps are numbered with Arabic numerals (1, 2, 3, etc.), chords are numbered with Roman numerals: I, II, III, etc.*

I   IImi   IIImi   IV   V   VImi   VII°   (VIII = I)

When describing chord progressions in words, Roman numerals are spoken as "one," "two," "three," etc., followed by the triad quality—e.g., "one major," "two minor," "three minor." and so on.

*There are various systems for numbering chords. In this book, we use all upper-case Roman numerals and identify quality by adding "mi" or "°", for minor and diminished chords, respectively. (Major chords are indicated by an upper-case Roman numeral alone, without a suffix.) Other systems use upper-case Roman numerals for major chord qualities and lower-case Roman numerals for minor chord qualities. Either system is acceptable as long as the quality of the triad is clearly identified.

The Diminished Triad

The seventh triad in the harmonized major scale is **diminished**. Diminished triads contain a **root**, **minor third**, and **diminished fifth**.

In the harmonized major scale, diminished triads occur only on the seventh scale degree, but they are also used in other ways that will be explored in later chapters.

As with major and minor triads, the best way to become familiar with the diminished triad is to sing its arpeggio.

EXERCISE 1

From any comfortable note, sing a minor triad arpeggio (1-♭3-5). From the perfect fifth, sing down a half step to the diminished fifth, then sing the root, minor third, and diminished fifth ascending and descending without the perfect fifth in between. Repeat this exercise from other pitches. Compare major, minor, and diminished arpeggios by singing them back-to-back from the same pitch:

1	3	5
1	♭3	5
1	♭3	♭5

EXERCISE 2

Sing the arpeggios of the harmonized major scale as follows:

1. Pick a tonic pitch in the lower part of your vocal range.
2. Starting on the tonic, sing the number of the root and a syllable—"la" is fine—for the third and fifth degrees of the chord, following this pattern up to the octave:

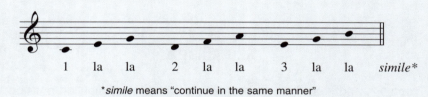

1   la   la   2   la   la   3   la   la   *simile**

*simile means "continue in the same manner"

3. Continue the pattern descending from the octave to the tonic:

8   la   la   7   la   la   6   la   la   *simile*

4. Practice singing the same pattern in a few other keys, then use this variation:

1   la   la   la   2   la   la   la   3   la   la   la   *simile*

Consonance and Dissonance

The sound of the diminished triad is quite different from major and minor triads, and it produces a different emotional response. In musical language, this difference is described by comparing each triad's relative degree of **consonance** (stability) or **dissonance** (activity). Consonant sounds are "restful," "pleasant," or "stable." This category includes major and minor triads as well as third, fourth, fifth, sixth, and octave intervals. Dissonant sounds are perceived as the opposite of consonant; that is, "tense," "unpleasant," and "unstable." These sounds include diminished triads as well as harmonic intervals of the second and seventh (an interval we've not yet explored).

Consonance and dissonance are subjective judgments rather than fixed dividing lines. The use of such negative terms as "tense" or "unpleasant" to describe dissonant sounds is somewhat deceptive; in fact, what may sound "tense" to one person may sound "energetic" or "fresh" to another. In popular music, dissonant sounds traditionally gravitate, or resolve, toward consonant sounds—as for example the dissonant VII° triad resolves to the consonant I major triad—but these rules are often broken in the search for new and surprising combinations of sound. Whatever your own tastes are, learning to recognize how musical structures evoke emotional responses is an important part of ear training.

Identifying Chord Progressions

Although chord progressions may seem more complicated than single-line melodies, the techniques for transcribing them are very much alike, as shown in the following exercise:

CD1 Track 17

EXERCISE 3

Listen to **CD1**, **Track 17**, and identify each progression using the following method:

1. Locate the tonic of the progression using the same method as for single-note melodies (on the CD, the tonic is played before each example).
2. Listen to the progression with your attention focused on the lowest note of each chord (the **bass line**).
3. Sing the bass line as you would any melody.
4. Figure out the scale step numbers of the bass notes and write them down using Roman numerals:

I   VI   IV   V   I

5. Once you have the bass line transcribed, add the triad qualities according to the scale harmony formula (i.e., all II chords are minor, all V chords are major, etc.):

I   VImi   IV   V   I

Often, musicians use numbers to communicate chord progressions even when they know the actual letter names of the chords because, unlike the letters, numbers also describe the relationships between chords. The amount of different chord combinations that occur regularly in popular music is relatively small, and a chord pattern such as "one-six-four-five," for example, is found in hundreds if not thousands of songs. One of the main goals of ear training is to move beyond hearing individual sounds and develop the ability to recognize larger patterns, and numbers provide an efficient way to organize and remember recurring sets of chords.

Chord Progressions:
Common Problems and Solutions

Chord progressions raise some particular ear training problems. These include:

1. **Matching pitch with low notes**

    As described in Chapter 1, when notes are too low to match in their actual pitch, you need to match pitch in another octave that's within your range. Practice matching pitch with bass notes by playing notes below your vocal range and singing them an octave or two higher, then apply the same technique to matching the roots of chords in a progression.

2. **Isolating the root of each chord**

    When analyzing a triad, higher or louder notes within the chord can sometimes distract you from hearing the root. Practice identifying and singing the roots of individual chords, as on CD1, Track 16. Returning to the progressions on Track 17, if you have a hard time hearing the root of a certain chord, hit "pause" immediately after the chord plays to isolate the sound (the "pitch freezing" method), then sing it using the same method. Once you have identified that particular root, listen to the progression again and sing it in context.

3. **Remembering groups of notes**

    You may get lost if you try to remember too many chords at once. Break the progression into smaller parts—two or three chords—and, when you're confident that you have figured out the separate parts, add them together into a single piece.

Chord progressions can seem very confusing at first because of the amount of information they contain, but after you've gained some experience you may be surprised at how few really different progressions there are in popular music, and how soon the common patterns become familiar.

Chord Charts

14

Chord charts are the most basic means of written communication between musicians. Whether consisting of a few chord symbols scribbled out on a scrap of paper or a complete part written out in great detail, chord charts allow any musician to learn, remember, and communicate progressions and rhythms.

Chord Symbols

Chord symbols are the standard means of describing harmony in contemporary popular music. For example, writing the letter "C" above the staff tells any musician on any instrument that the chord is a C major triad. Although a chord symbol doesn't contain details about fingering or voicing, every musician reading and playing that chord symbol will play the same chord quality.

Every chord symbol needs to communicate two things: 1) the letter name of the root of the chord and 2) its quality. So far, we've learned four chord types, each with its own symbol:

Chord type	Symbol	Examples
Major triad	letter name alone	C, A, F♯
Minor triad	letter name followed by "mi"	Cmi, Gmi, E♭mi
Diminished triad	letter name followed by "°"	C°, D°, G♯°
Power chord	letter name followed by "5"	C5, E5, B♭5

Often, musicians use shorthand symbols for certain chord types, such as a minus sign to indicate a minor quality ("C-"), but these symbols are not always consistent and can cause problems when musicians with different levels of training and experience read from the same chart. As a rule, use the clearest, simplest chord symbols at all times, as indicated above.

Rhythmic (Slash) Notation

Rhythms have the same value regardless of whether they're referring to single notes or to chords, but there are differences in notation. Rather than indicating a certain pitch, rhythmic notation shows how to play the group of notes indicated by the chord symbol above the staff. In rhythmic (a.k.a. slash) notation, stems remain the same while slashes or diamonds replace the standard noteheads, as follows:

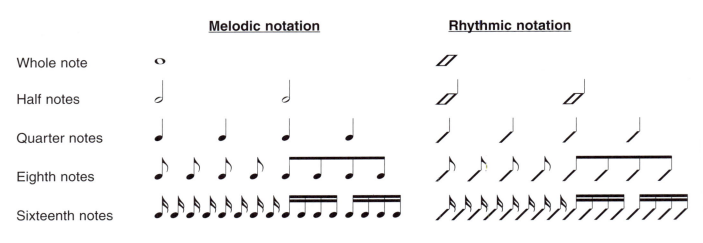

	Melodic notation	Rhythmic notation
Whole note		
Half notes		
Quarter notes		
Eighth notes		
Sixteenth notes		

Both the slashes and the diamonds are positioned directly on the center of the staff. Dots and ties are also used the same way in both melodic notation and rhythmic notation. Below is a typical example of chord chart notation:

Transcribing Chord Progressions

The method for transcribing chord progressions into chord chart form actually involves three steps: 1) transcribing the rhythm, 2) identifying the chords, and 3) putting them together on the staff.

CD1 Track 18   **EXERCISE 1**

Listen to **CD1**, **Track 18**, and follow these steps as you transcribe each chord progression in rhythm (use a pencil and have an eraser handy):

1. Write the time signature on the staff. Count the number of bars in the example, and draw the bar lines on the staff:

2. Using the same techniques you've learned for transcribing melodic rhythms, transcribe the chord rhythms and write them on the staff using rhythmic notation.

3. Using the same techniques you've learned for identifying chords, write the chord symbols above the staff. (All progressions are in the key of C.) It is very important to position each chord symbol directly above the rhythm where it first occurs—a general rule about transcription is that the music should look the way it sounds; so if a chord occurs on the "and of 4," the symbol should be positioned directly above that spot. If the same chord is played several times in a row, the symbol only needs to appear the first time:

Melody and Harmony

15

Y ou've learned the major scale and how it can be used as the source of melodies. The same idea works for chords—if you break the notes of a chord down and play them one at a time, they form a melody of sorts (technically, an arpeggio). Analysis of typical melodies shows that note choices in general, and melodic intervals in particular, tend to be related to arpeggios, or **chord tones**, of the harmony behind them. Training your ear to recognize these relationships will improve your ability to understand both melodic patterns and chord structures.

Chord Tones as Melodies

When you learned melodic intervals in Chapter 10, each was described in relation to a well-known melody (e.g., major sixth ascending = "My Bonnie Lies Over the Ocean"). Looking at each of these intervals in a harmonic context reveals that they are built from chord tones; that is, the major sixth in "My Bonnie" is not just *any* sixth, but specifically the interval between the fifth and the major third of a major triad. In fact, the arpeggio of a major triad contains every one of the consonant intervals—major and minor thirds and sixths, as well as perfect fourths, fifths, and octaves.

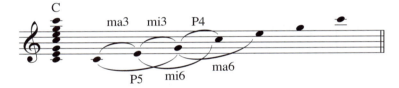

EXERCISE 1

The following melodies each contain only the chord tones of a C major triad. Play C on a guitar or piano and sightsing the melodies by relative pitch.

Melodies consisting only of the notes of a single triad are limited, often sounding like bugle calls, but when tones from several chords—**I**, **IV**, and **V**, in particular—are combined, the results can be much more "melodic." Between them, the tones of these three chords include all of the notes of the major scale.

Chapter 15

EXERCISE 2

Slowly sing the C major scale while playing the major triad shown above each note:

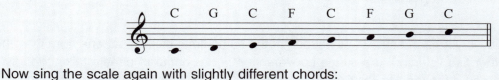

Now sing the scale again with slightly different chords:

Changing the chord behind the last note from C to F has a profound effect on the feeling of the melody. Rather than finishing with a sense of strength and finality (i.e., resolving), the melody is left "hanging"—even though it's the tonic of the scale. Any given note in a melody is related at the same time to both the scale of the key and the structure of the chord accompanying it, and by becoming aware of the interaction between all three, you will improve your ability to understand music in its entirety, not just as separate elements.

CD1 Track 19

EXERCISE 3

CD1, **Track 19** contains melodies based on I, IV, and V chords in the key of C, with accompaniment. Listen and follow these steps as you transcribe each example:

1. Listen for the chord changes (I, IV, or V). The bass plays roots, while the keyboard plays chords above. Write the chord symbols above the staff in their approximate location:

2. Transcribe the melody onto the staff.

3. Below each note, write its scale step number.

4. Below the scale step numbers, write the number that indicates the relationship of the note to the under lying chord, i.e., 1, 3, or 5:

Nursery rhythms, folk songs, anthems, and religious music, to name a few universal styles, are filled with melodic examples like these—for more practice, pick some and analyze them for chord/scale relationships.

16 Transcribing Melody, Harmony, and Rhythm

When melody, rhythm, and chords all happen at the same time, picking out one from the other two is rather like listening to a single conversation in a roomful of people talking loudly; it takes focused attention. So far, you've worked with these elements in pairs—melody with rhythm, harmony with rhythm, and melody with harmony. Now it's time to learn how to transcribe when all three occur together.

Before getting into the CD examples, we'll add one more element that is important to natural musical phrasing...

Pickup Notes

Songs often begin with a note or two that precede the main part of the melody. A good example is "Happy Birthday," where the word "happy" precedes the downbeat on "<u>birth</u>-day." Notes that precede the downbeat of a phrase are commonly called **pickup notes** (or "pickup phrases," or simply "pickups"). A pickup consists of one or more notes that occur during the count-off (the bar before the downbeat). This bar is counted normally, although in printed music the rests before the pickup are commonly omitted and only the pickup melody itself is notated.

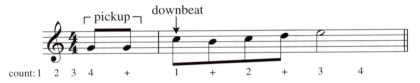

count: 1   2   3   4   +   1   +   2   +   3   4

CD1 Track 20

EXERCISE 1

CD1, **Track 20** contains major melodies with diatonic harmony, in various keys. The tonic is played before each example. Listen and follow these steps as you transcribe:

1. Listen to the example. Determine the meter and length, then lay out the clef, key signature (if other than C major), time signature, and bar lines on the staff:

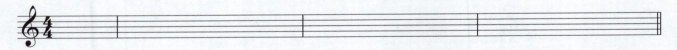

2. Using the techniques you've already learned for transcribing melody combined with rhythm, write the melody on the staff with correct notation:

Chapter 16

3. Using the techniques you've already learned for transcribing chords, write the chord symbols above the staff. Since the melody is already on the staff, there is no need for specific rhythmic notation—whatever beat or part of a beat a chord occurs on, write the chord symbol directly above it:

4. Now that the example is completely notated, visualize how you will play the melody on your instrument —where your hands will be and what fingering to use—then actually play it. If you have visualized accurately, the melody will fall under your fingers and you will play it correctly the first time. Using the same method, visualize and play the chords. Visualization is an important bridge between the concept of ear training and its practical application to your playing.

If you find it particularly difficult to separate and/or identify rhythm, melody, and chords, go back and review Tracks 1-4 (melodies), Track 17 (triad progressions), and Track 19 (melodies over I, IV, and V chords), then come back to this exercise.

Major Key Signatures & Chords

Some of the examples in this chapter are in keys other than C major—be sure to use the proper key signatures and diatonic chords. If you're not familiar with these, the following reference may prove useful.

Keys ↓	I	IImi	IIImi	IV	V	VImi	VII°
C major	C	Dmi	Emi	F	G	Ami	B°
G major	G	Ami	Bmi	C	D	Emi	F#°
D major	D	Emi	F#mi	G	A	Bmi	C#°
A major	A	Bmi	C#mi	D	E	F#mi	G#°
E major	E	F#mi	G#mi	A	B	C#mi	D#°
B major	B	C#mi	D#mi	E	F#	G#mi	A#°
F major	F	Gmi	Ami	B♭	C	Dmi	E°
B♭ major	B♭	Cmi	Dmi	E♭	F	Gmi	A°
E♭ major	E♭	Fmi	Gmi	A♭	B♭	Cmi	D°
A♭ major	A♭	B♭mi	Cmi	D♭	E♭	Fmi	G°
D♭ major	D♭	E♭mi	Fmi	G♭	A♭	B♭mi	C°

Part II
Minor Tonality

From matching pitch to transcribing melody, harmony, and rhythm, Part I was a major step forward in your ear training skills. In Part II, the sounds will change but the fundamental techniques for learning them will stay the same.

Like its major counterpart, **minor tonality** is a complete system of melodies, chords, and progressions that plays a significant role in popular music. Major and minor tonalities share the same intervals and chords, and the same ear training techniques still apply. With the foundation you've laid so far, your rate of progress will increase, and you'll be able to absorb new sounds ever more quickly.

The Natural Minor Scale

17

In the simplest terms, there are two primary emotional qualities in music: major and minor. The major quality, as heard in the major scale, is almost universally perceived as "bright" or "happy," and forms the basis of melodies in a great variety of styles. The minor quality, on the other hand, is usually perceived as "dark" or "sad," a quality reflected in the **natural minor scale**.

Relative Minor

Consider a C major scale, with its whole- and half- step formula:

W	W	H	W	W	W	H
C	D	E	F	G	A	B	C

What if the same scale steps were sung or played, but starting from a different note in the series—for example, starting and ending on the 6th scale degree? The result would be a pattern like this:

W	H	W	W	H	W	W
A	B	C	D	E	F	G	A

This is in fact, the **relative minor** of C major, the A natural minor scale—so called, because it is a minor scale that derives "naturally," without alterations, from the major scale.

Although the natural minor scale can be derived from the major scale by starting on the 6th scale step of any major scale pattern, it's more musical to think of it as its own tonality—with its own tonic and its own scale step pattern—so this is how we'll learn it.

The Minor Third

The essential difference between major and minor tonalities in the quality of the third scale degree: while the major scale contains a major third scale degree, the natural minor scale contains a **minor third** scale degree—also called a flat 3rd.

EXERCISE 1

Sing the triad arpeggios, then sing the scale segments.

NOTE: When singing minor thirds, you don't need to sing the words "flat three"—just sing "three," and let the pitch reflect the quality.

The Minor Sixth and Seventh

The natural minor scale also contains two other notes that differ from the major scale—a **minor sixth** and a **minor seventh**. Like the minor third, each of these notes is a half step below the equivalent major scale degree.

Along with the minor third, the minor sixth and seventh scale degrees contribute to the overall effect of the minor tonality (a feeling usually described as "sad" or "dark"). Compare major and minor melodies that emphasize the sixth and seventh degrees one after the other and you can easily hear the differences.

EXERCISE 2

1. From any comfortable note, sing this major scale melody:

1   2   3   4   5   6   5

2. Eliminate "2" and "4" and sing the remaining notes (a major triad plus the major sixth):

1   3   5   6   5

3. Now, sing the first six degrees of the <u>natural minor</u> scale:

1   2   ♭3   4   5   ♭6   5

4. Eliminate "2" and "4," and sing the remaining notes (a minor triad plus the minor sixth):

1   ♭3   5   ♭6   5

5. Now, try a descending pattern. First, sing these <u>major</u> scale tones:

8   7   6   5   6   7   8

6. Now, sing these <u>natural minor</u> scale tones:

8   ♭7   ♭6   5   ♭6   ♭7   8

EXERCISE 3

Sing complete natural minor scales ascending and descending from random pitches.

CD2 Track 1

EXERCISE 4

CD2, Track 1 is designed to test your knowledge of the natural minor scale. You'll hear the entire scale played ascending or descending followed by a single note from the scale—identify the correct scale degree by singing the scale from the tonic or octave and counting steps until you match pitch.

Minor Melodies
18

All of the principles for identifying melodies and intervals within the natural minor scale are the same as for the major scale, and you can learn them through the same types of singing and transcription exercises.

Pitch Memory and Pattern Recognition

Accurate transcription depends on the combination of two skills: pitch memory and pattern recognition. **Pitch memory** is your ability to remember melodic phrases, an ability you demonstrate every time you sing a song in your head. **Pattern recognition** is your ability to relate groups of notes to a larger structure, such as the major or minor scale. This is the skill that turns pitch memory into a usable musical tool—if you understand the patterns that make up melodies, you can learn, remember, and play them much more effectively. These skills are the same for both major and minor melodies.

CD2 Track 2

EXERCISE 1

CD2, Track 2 contains natural minor melodies. Follow these steps to transcribe each example by scale step number:

1. Listen to the tonic as it's played. Sing "1," and then sing the complete minor scale to familiarize your ear with that key.

2. While the example plays the first time, count the number of pitches, and draw a short blank on your answer sheet for each pitch in the melody, like this:

    ＿＿＿ ＿＿＿ ＿＿＿ ＿＿＿ ＿＿＿ ＿＿＿ ＿＿＿

3. On the appropriate blanks, write down any notes that you recognize right away, such as the "1's". You don't have to transcribe the notes in order—you might recognize the first and third note of the melody, say, before you recognize the other notes. Writing those notes down will clear the way for you to concentrate on the less familiar notes:

    __1__ ＿＿＿ __1__ ＿＿＿ ＿＿＿ ＿＿＿ ＿＿＿

4. To identify less familiar pitches, use the "pitch freezing" method that was introduced for major scales:
    * Before you play the example, sing "1."
    * Hit "play," and sing along with the example until you reach the first note you don't know.
    * Immediately pause the CD, then sing the scale between "1" and the "unknown tone," counting the steps along the way.

   If your pitch matching and scale singing are accurate, you will be able to identify the correct scale step:

    __1__ __♭3__ __1__ ＿＿＿ ＿＿＿ ＿＿＿ ＿＿＿

5. Repeat this procedure for each of the remaining pitches:

    __1__ __♭3__ __1__ __5__ __♭6__ __4__ __5__

6.   After you transcribe the phrase, play it on your instrument—the tonic/key is identified for you at the start of each example—and see if it matches the sound you are hearing. If you've missed any notes, work on the melody some more. Once you've accurately transcribed a phrase, move on and give yourself another challenge. As your pitch memory and pattern recognition improve, you will find yourself identifying entire phrases rather than separate notes.

Transcribe for about fifteen minutes a day until you've finished all of the examples.

Minor Key Signatures

The process of transcribing melodies in musical notation is the same for minor keys as for major. Since minor keys have their own key signatures, there is no need to use accidentals in front of the minor third, sixth, or seventh.

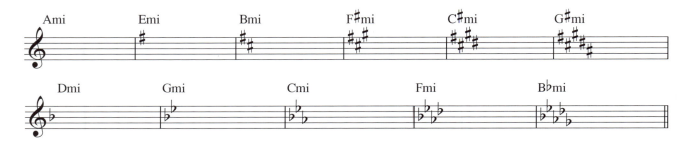

It may help you to remember that every minor key shares a key signature with its relative major—e.g., A minor/C major (no sharps or flats), E minor/G major (1 sharp), D minor/F major (1 flat), etc. To find the relative major of a minor scale, count up to its 3rd scale step.

NOTE: The term "flat" is often used to mean "lowered" or "minor" (i.e., "flat third" is a convenient way to say "lowered third" or "minor third"), but in some keys a note is lowered by removing a sharp sign, not by adding a flat sign. To avoid confusion, get in the habit of saying "lowered" or "minor" instead of "flat."

CD2 Track 2

EXERCISE 2

Transcribe the same melodies from **CD2, Track 2**, this time writing the pitches and rhythms on the staff. As before, separate the rhythm and melody from each other, break the phrase into its parts, and reassemble it on the staff (see Chapter 7 if you need to review this).

Sixteenth-Note Rhythms

19

The sixteenth note is the smallest division of the beat ordinarily found in popular music, and certain styles, such as funk, are based primarily on sixteenth-note rhythms. The same methods that you used to learn eighth-note rhythms—starting with short phrases and gradually building in length and complexity—also apply to sixteenth notes. Learning short phrases is the first step toward mastering real-world rhythms.

Counting Sixteenth Notes

To locate any given sixteenth note exactly within a bar or a beat, you need a consistent method of counting and verbalizing sixteenth notes. The commonly accepted method is to assign the following syllables to each sixteenth note within a beat:

"**One** - ee - and - uh, **two** - ee - and - uh..." *simile*

The numbers represent the downbeats, the *ands* fall on the upbeats, and the *ee* and *uh* represent the sixteenths in between. When notated, it is common to use the letter "**e**" for the sound *ee* and the letter "**a**" for the sound *uh*, with *and* represented by the symbol "**+**" or "**&**."

1   e   +   a   2   e   +   a   *simile*

With these numbers and syllables, you can verbally describe the exact location of any sixteenth note. For example, the fourth sixteenth note of the first beat is called "the *a* (pronounced *uh*) of 1," and the second sixteenth note of the second beat is called "the *e* (pronounced *ee*) of 2."

One-Beat Combinations

Because there are four sixteenth notes in one beat of 4/4 meter, a single beat has the same number of possible rhythmic combinations as two beats of eighth notes (sixteenth-note rhythmic phrases sound like eighth-note phrases played twice as fast). There are fourteen unique sixteenth-note/rest combinations.

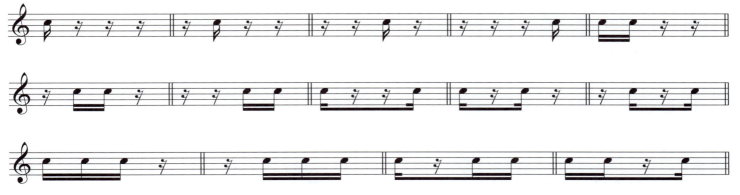

CD2 Track 3

EXERCISE 1

The technique for transcribing sixteenth notes is the same as for transcribing eighth notes, but with twice as many notes per beat. Listen to **CD2**, **Track 3**, and transcribe each one-beat example following these steps:

1. Above the staff, make a small mark for each possible sixteenth note or rest (in a one-beat phrase, there are four possible sixteenth notes):

2. Tap your foot in time with the meter (quarter notes), listen to the example, and sing along. Memorize the phrase quickly, and then sing it back to yourself. Once it is memorized, slow it down with your voice. While singing the rhythm, tap your finger or a pencil in steady sixteenths and whenever you make a sound, place a dot on the staff beneath the sixteenth where it occurs (the "dot-tap" method):

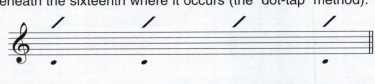

3. Fill in the appropriate note and rest values (determine the sustain of each note as accurately as you can, but remember that notating the correct attack is more important):

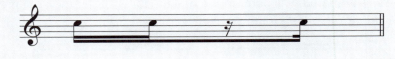

Two- and Four-Beat Phrases

The same principle of counting applies to two-beat and four-beat phrases, and just like one-beat phrases, longer phrases become familiar with practice. Although the rhythms may extend across beats, they should be notated so that *each beat is clearly visible*. If a note is held across a beat, use a tie rather than a single, longer note value, and beam the notes within each beat together. For example, the phrase below can be much more easily read when beams and ties are used to keep each beat visible:

After you transcribe the examples on the CD, compare your notation with the standard notation shown in the Answer Key, and edit your written version to match.

CD2 Track 4

EXERCISE 2

CD2, **Track 4** contains two-beat and four-beat sixteenth-note phrases for transcription.

Minor Melodies with Sixteenth-Note Rhythms

20

earning sixteenth-note rhythms apart from melodies allowed you to concentrate on each sound individually without distractions; the next step is to combine them into typical musical phrases.

The method for transcribing melodies with sixteenth-note rhythms is the same as that for melodies with eighth-note rhythms.

CD2 Track 5

EXERCISE 1

Listen to **CD2**, **Track 5**, and follow these steps as you transcribe each melody on the staff (use a pencil—not a pen—and have an eraser handy):

1. Identify the tonic and meter. Write the clef, key signature, and time signature on the staff and lay out the proper number of bars, providing plenty of room for each one.

2. Listen to the example all the way through and memorize it. If the example is too long to memorize all at once, work on shorter segments. Sing along with the melody and rhythm until you know it.

3. Below the staff, lightly pencil in the rhythm of the notes. Use proper spacing. When you're done, check the rhythms against the actual musical example to confirm their accuracy:

4. Above each rhythm, write a dot on the staff for the pitch of each note. Again, check for accuracy:

5. Add the rhythmic notation to the notes on the staff, and erase the rhythmic sketch below the staff. The example is now complete. Check it again and sightsing it to confirm the accuracy of the notes and rhythms:

Transcription is not intended to be a sterile exercise; it's one of the most useful and rewarding skills a musician can develop. Of course, the examples in this book are carefully arranged for the step-by-step development of specific skills, while "real" music happens all at once with no regard for your particular skill level. But don't wait until your skills are perfected before you begin transcribing the music you like, regardless of style or complexity. If you've been following the steps in this method faithfully, there is already a great amount of music well within your grasp.

Minor-Key Triad
21 Progressions

The relationship between diatonic melodies and chord progressions is the same in minor keys as it is in major—the roots of all the chords belong to the scale, and the qualities of the chords always follow the same pattern regardless of key.

The Harmonized Natural Minor Scale

Natural minor scale harmonies are built just as they are in major keys—notes of the scale are stacked on top of one another in third intervals to produce a series of triads, resulting in a harmonized scale. The order of triad qualities in the harmonized minor scale is shown below:

Imi   II°   ♭III   IVmi   Vmi   ♭VI   ♭VII   Imi

NOTE: In this book, we use flats ("♭III," "♭VI," "♭VII") to highlight the degrees of the minor scale that differ from major (lowered third, sixth, and seventh). This style of notation applies to numeral systems only—on the staff, major and minor scales are each notated by means of their own respective key signatures.

EXERCISE 1

Sing the arpeggios of the harmonized natural minor scale as follows:

1. Pick a tonic in the lower part of your vocal range, and sing a one-octave natural minor scale ascending and descending.
2. Starting on the tonic chord ("one"), sing the number of the root and the syllable "la" for the third and fifth degrees of the chord, following this pattern up to the octave:

3. Continue the pattern descending from the octave to the tonic:

4. Sing this pattern from other tonics, then use this variation:

Chapter 21

Transcribing by Number

The steps used for transcribing minor-key progressions are the same as those you've already learned for major-key progressions.

CD2 Track 6

EXERCISE 2

Listen to **CD2**, **Track 6**, and follow these steps as you transcribe each progression:

1. Identify the tonic note of the key, and sing the minor scale to "tune up" your ear.
2. Count the number of chords in the progression and write down a blank for each chord:

   ___   ___   ___   ___   ___

3. Fill in the scale step number and quality for any chords that are immediately recognizable, whether or not they are in order. Remember that since we're dealing with diatonic progressions, the chord quality built on each scale step never varies.

   __Imi__   ___   ___   ___   __Imi__

4. To identify each unknown chord, sing the minor scale from the tonic of the key to the root of the chord and count scale steps, the same as you would to identify a melody. Once you locate the root, the chord quality follows automatically. Write down the Roman numeral and quality for each chord:

   __Imi__   __IVmi__   __♭III__   __♭VII__   __Imi__

5. To check your work, sing the root progression as you transcribed it along with the recording to see if the pitches match. Review any that don't.

Diatonic Chords in Minor Keys

The following reference may prove useful as you continue to transcribe chord progressions in minor keys. If you are unfamiliar with the chords in a particular key, transcribe by numbers first, and then convert the numbers to letter names.

Keys ↓	Imi	II°	♭III	IVmi	Vmi	♭VI	♭VII
A minor	Ami	B°	C	Dmi	Emi	F	G
E minor	Emi	F♯°	G	Ami	Bmi	C	D
B minor	Bmi	C♯°	D	Emi	F♯mi	G	A
F♯ minor	F♯mi	G♯°	A	Bmi	C♯mi	D	E
C♯ minor	C♯mi	D♯°	E	F♯mi	G♯mi	A	B
G♯ minor	G♯mi	A♯°	B	C♯mi	D♯mi	E	F♯
D minor	Dmi	E°	F	Gmi	Ami	B♭	C
G minor	Gmi	A°	B♭	Cmi	Dmi	E♭	F
C minor	Cmi	D°	E♭	Fmi	Gmi	A♭	B♭
F minor	Fmi	G°	A♭	B♭mi	Cmi	D♭	E♭
B♭ minor	B♭mi	C°	D♭	E♭mi	Fmi	G♭	A♭

22 Minor-Key Progressions with Rhythm

I n this chapter, you'll combine diatonic minor-key triad progressions with sixteenth-note rhythms and transcribe them on the staff using rhythmic notation.

Transcription Review

In Chapter 14, you learned how to transcribe diatonic major-key progressions and eighth-note rhythms using rhythmic notation. Although you're now working with minor-key progressions and sixteenth notes rhythms, the method is the same.

CD2 Track 7

EXERCISE 1

CD2, **Track 7** contains triad progressions in the key of A minor. Listen and follow these steps for each example:

1. **Transcribe the rhythms.** Write the rhythmic figures on the staff in their proper locations with the appropriate notation.

2. **Identify the chords.** Use the techniques already discussed for identifying the bass line and chord qualities:

When you notate progressions including sixteenth-note rhythms, it's especially important to locate the chord symbols precisely above the point where they first occur. A good practice is to make the notation as clear as you'd want it to be if you were reading it yourself for the first time. Look at professionally copied music as a guide for notation, spacing, and overall clarity. It takes extra time to write clearly, but the extra effort will lead to much better musical results.

Minor-Key Melodies with Harmony and Rhythm

In this chapter, you'll transcribe minor-key melodies, harmony, and sixteenth-note rhythms. Back in Chapter 16, you transcribed major-key melody, harmony, and eighth-note rhythms—the specific musical ingredients have changed, but the methods are the same.

CD2 Track 8

EXERCISE 1

Listen to **CD2**, **Track 8**, and transcribe each minor-key melody using the following method:

1. Listen to the example, and determine its meter, key, and length. Lay out the clef, key signature, time signature, and bar lines on the staff:

2. Using the techniques you've already learned for transcribing rhythms, sketch the rhythms under the staff. Take it one beat at a time and keep every beat visible, using ties where necessary. Mark the attacks first, then listen for sustain; be sure that the total combined value of notes and rests in each bar matches the time signature exactly:

3. Using the techniques you've learned for transcribing melody, write the melody on the staff with correct notation and combine it with the rhythm:

4. Use the techniques you've learned for transcribing chords, and write the chord symbols above the staff. Since the melody is already on the staff, there is no need for specific rhythmic notation—whatever beat or part of a beat a chord occurs on, write the chord symbol directly above it:

5. Now that the example is completely notated, visualize how you'll play the melody on your instrument—where your hands will be and what fingering you'll use—then actually play it. If you have visualized correctly, the melody will fall under your fingers and you will play it correctly the first time. Using the same method, visualize and play the chords. To turn the concepts of ear training into practical tools, you must constantly reinforce the connection between your ears, brain, and hands.

Part III
Seventh Chords and Blues

You've completed your study of diatonic major and minor melody and harmony, a world in which rules are strict and relationships are predictable. Reality is, unfortunately, rarely that tidy—even the least complicated blues, funk, or rock song routinely includes sounds that fall outside the diatonic framework.

But even when the rules are being stretched or broken, diatonic systems remain the underlying structures of popular music, and the patterns you hear from this point forward will be mostly variations or combinations of what you have already learned.

Seventh Intervals and Seventh Chords

24

The harmonies of certain styles of music—notably blues, jazz, and funk/R&B—are based not on triads but on **seventh chords**, which are formed by adding **seventh intervals** to triads. First, let's look at seventh intervals in more detail.

Seventh Intervals

There are three seventh interval qualities:

> **major seventh:**   one half step below an octave
> **minor seventh:**   one half step below the major seventh
> **diminished seventh:**   one half step below the minor seventh

Sevenths are rarely heard as melodic intervals because, being large and comparatively dissonant, they are difficult to sing accurately. As harmonic intervals, though, major and minor sevenths in particular are very common (the diminished seventh interval will be explored later, in Chapter 35).

EXERCISE 1

1. Sing a major scale from the tonic to the octave, descend one scale step to the seventh, and then sing the tonic and seventh alone. This is a *major seventh* interval. Major sevenths are easiest to hear and sing in relation to the octave, rather than the tonic, because the octave and major seventh are only a half step apart.
2. Next, sing a *minor* scale up to the octave, go back to the seventh, and then sing the tonic and minor seventh scale degree back-to-back. This is a *minor seventh* interval.
3. Finally, sing major and minor sevenths consecutively from various notes, using the octave as a reference.

The most commonly cited example of a melody featuring a major seventh interval—"(Somewhere) Over the Rainbow"—begins with a tonic-octave-major seventh combination. Minor seventh intervals are even more rare, with probably the best-known example being the first two notes of the main theme from the film and television series *Star Trek*.

CD2 Track 9

EXERCISE 2

CD2, Track 9 contains major and minor seventh harmonic intervals for identification. Listen, sing the notes separately, then identify the quality.

Diatonic Seventh Chords

When major or minor seventh intervals are added to diatonic triads, four diatonic seventh chord qualities result:

triad quality	+	seventh interval	=	seventh chord
major triad		major seventh		major seventh chord
major triad		minor seventh		dominant seventh chord
minor triad		minor seventh		minor seventh chord
diminished triad		minor seventh		minor seven flat-five chord

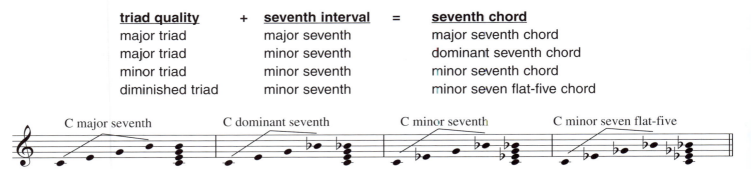

Of the four diatonic seventh chord qualities, three (major seventh, minor seventh, and minor seven flat-five) share the qualities of the underlying major, minor, and diminished triads. The fourth quality, dominant, has a distinctly different structure—the combination of tones creates an internal dissonance that gives the dominant seventh chord an "unsettled" quality.

EXERCISE 3

Sing each of the diatonic seventh chord qualities as an arpeggio. Start from any comfortable note and follow this method:

1. **Major seventh chord**
   - sing a <u>major</u> triad
   - sing a <u>major</u> seventh interval
   - combine the major triad with the major seventh: 1 – 3 – 5 – 7
2. **Dominant seventh chord**
   - sing a <u>major</u> triad
   - sing a <u>minor</u> seventh interval
   - combine the major triad with the minor seventh: 1 – 3 – 5 – ♭7
3. **Minor seventh chord**
   - sing a <u>minor</u> triad
   - sing a <u>minor</u> seventh interval
   - combine the minor triad with the minor seventh: 1 – ♭3 – 5 – ♭7
4. **Minor seven flat-five chord**
   - sing a <u>diminished</u> triad
   - sing a <u>minor</u> seventh interval
   - combine the diminished triad with the minor seventh: 1 – ♭3 – ♭5 – ♭7

After you can sing the four seventh chord qualities separately, sing them all back to back from the same note. When you sing them in the order shown, each chord differs from the previous by only a single note.

Chapter 24

Identifying Diatonic Seventh Chords

Singing seventh chords as arpeggios gives you an understanding of the structure of each chord, but hearing the notes played all at once reveals their true musical qualities. The "happy-sad-dissonant" comparison that helped distinguish major, minor, and diminished triads becomes a little more complex when sevenths are added. Major sevenths are often described as "sweet" and minor sevenths as "dark" (each being "restful" in its own way), while the dominant seventh and minor seven flat-five chords are more or less "unsettled." These subjective impressions help you recognize chords in comparison to each other, but you also need a method for analyzing their structures.

CD2 Track 10

EXERCISE 4

Listen to **CD2**, **Track 10** as you follow these steps for identifying seventh chord qualities (the root is always the lowest note):

1. **Describe your subjective impression of the sound.** Is it sweet? Dark? Unsettled? Remember your first impression as you follow the rest of these steps.
2. **Locate the root** (the lowest note), and match pitch.
3. **Identify the quality of the third.** From the root, sing up two scale steps to the third scale degree while the chord sustains. You don't need to consciously try to sing a major or minor scale—just let your voice blend with the chord until it sounds in tune, then stop and identify the quality of the scale degree you're singing (major or minor).
4. **Identify the quality of the fifth.** Sing from the root up to the fifth scale degree, matching pitch with the sound of the chord and then identifying the quality. Is it a perfect fifth? Out of the four diatonic seventh chord qualities, only one has a diminished fifth, so if the fifth is not perfect, it can only be a minor seven flat-five chord. If the fifth is perfect, go on to the next step.
5. **Identify the quality of the seventh.** Sing the root of the chord, sing the octave, and then let your voice travel down until you match pitch with the seventh degree of the chord. After you have a match, stop and identify the quality of the seventh interval, which will be either a half step or a whole step below the octave.
6. **Add up the interval qualities** to determine the chord quality. Compare it to your first impression, associating your subjective feelings with the sound of the chord structure. With some experience, your "impressions" will no longer be subjective—they will be reliable indicators of chord quality.

Repeat this exercise as needed until you're able to identify the different seventh chord qualities with accuracy.

Diatonic Seventh Chord Progressions

25

 iatonic progressions containing seventh chords require no special transcription techniques beyond those that you have already used for diatonic triad progressions. While the chord qualities are more complex, the root movement is the same.

Major-Key Progressions

The order of seventh chord qualities in the harmonized major scale is as follows:

Ima7   IImi7   IIImi7   IVma7   V7   VImi7   VIImi7(♭5)

Comparing major scale seventh chord harmonies to triad harmonies:

Scale degree	Triad quality	Seventh chord quality
I	major	major seventh
II	minor	minor seventh
III	minor	minor seventh
IV	major	major seventh
V	major	dominant seventh
VI	minor	minor seventh
VII	diminished	minor seven flat-five

With the exception of the dominant seventh chord (the V chord), which has a clearly different quality, the other seventh chord qualities are essentially more complex versions of their corresponding triads.

EXERCISE 1

Sing the harmonized major scale using seventh arpeggios. Begin by singing the arpeggio of the Ima7 chord ascending and descending, then the arpeggio of the IImi7 chord, the IIImi7 chord, and so on through the scale as shown here:

The function of each chord and the general ways in which chords are arranged into progressions remain the same for seventh chords as they do for triads. The differences have mostly to do with how these chords are applied stylistically; for example, rock harmony is built primarily on triads while jazz, blues, and R&B favor seventh chords and their relatives.

Chapter 25

CD2 Track 11

EXERCISE 2

CD2, **Track 11** contains diatonic major-key progressions with seventh chords. Transcribe the progressions following the same steps that you used for triad progressions, i.e., locate the root of each chord, identify its scale position, and name its quality. Since these progressions are all diatonic, the chord quality for each scale degree is predetermined.

Minor-Key Progressions

The order of seventh chords in the harmonized natural minor scale is as follows:

Imi7   IImi7(♭5)   ♭IIIma7   IVmi7   Vmi7   ♭VIma7   ♭VII7

Comparing minor scale seventh chord harmonies to triad harmonies:

Scale degree	Triad quality	Seventh chord quality
I	minor	minor seventh
II	diminished	minor seven flat-five
♭III	major	major seventh
IV	minor	minor seventh
V	minor	minor seventh
♭VI	major	major seventh
♭VII	major	dominant seventh

EXERCISE 3

Sing the harmonized natural minor scale using the arpeggio of each chord as shown below:

CD2 Track 12

EXERCISE 4

CD2, **Track 12** contains diatonic minor-key progressions with seventh chords. Transcribe the progressions following the same steps that you used for minor-key triad progressions.

Triplet Rhythms

26

We've studied rhythms that divide the beat into two parts (eighth notes) and four parts (sixteenth notes). The other common rhythmic division of the beat is into *three* equal parts, called a **triplet**.

The most common triplets are based on eighth notes (eighth-note triplets), sixteenth notes (sixteenth-note triplets), and quarter notes (quarter-note triplets); in each case, a triplet occupies the same amount of time occupied by two non-triplet notes of the same value (e.g., three triplet eighth notes occupy the same amount of time as two "normal" eighth notes). Triplets also form the rhythmic basis of some very common styles, including shuffle and swing.

Eighth-Note Triplets

Triplets have a unique quality that is distinct from rhythms that divide the beat in two. The most important thing to remember about triplets is that *all three notes are exactly equal in length*. Eighth notes divide a beat exactly in two, and an eighth-note triplet divides a beat into exactly three parts. Eighth-note triplets are beamed and labeled with the number "3" to clearly set them apart from ordinary eighth notes.

By contrast, none of the following rhythms are triplets even though all include three notes in the space of a single beat because the notes are *not* all of equal value:

EXERCISE 1

At a slow-to-medium tempo, clap a bar of eighth notes and a bar of eighth-note triplets alternately. It is helpful to count out loud as you clap—sing "*one-and-two-and*," etc. for the eighth notes and "*one-and-uh, two-and-uh*" for the triplets. Go back and forth between the two rhythms until the transition from one to the other is quick and accurate. As you change from one rhythm to the next, notice how different they feel. Eighth notes feel "straight" or "square" while triplets are often described as "round" or "rolling." These subjective feelings are very important in helping you to recognize and transcribe mixed rhythms in a piece of music.

As with eighth and sixteenth notes, various combinations of notes and rests within a triplet create different phrases. When you clap the following rhythms, continue to count all three notes of the triplet, including rests:

Sixteenth-Note Triplets

Sixteenth-note triplets have the same relationship to sixteenth notes that eighth-note triplets have to eighth notes. Each sixteenth-note triplet occupies the space of two normal sixteenth notes, and two sixteenth-note triplets occupy a single beat of 4/4 meter.

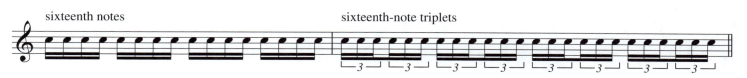

EXERCISE 2

Clap and sing sixteenth notes and sixteenth-note triplets, alternately. Since there are twice as many sixteenth notes per beat as there are eighth notes, even at a slower tempo it's hard to sing fast enough to match the rhythm. Instead of counting the triplets with numbers, use an easy-to-sing sound:

"one - ee - and - uh, two - ee - and - uh, dih - duh - lee, dih - duh - lee, dih - duh - lee, dih - duh - lee"

When rhythms are mixed, make a smooth transition from phrase to phrase without stopping or altering the beat. Play the following rhythms on your instrument:

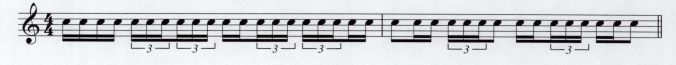

Quarter-Note Triplets

Quarter-note triplets are another triplet variation. Quarter-note triplets are notated by the number "3" surrounded by brackets:

EXERCISE 3

To count quarter-note triplets, begin by singing eighth-note triplets and placing an accent on every second eighth note (tap your foot on every downbeat while you sing the accents—this may take some time to master):

one and *uh* two *and* ah *three* and *uh* four *and* ah

When you leave out the unaccented eighth notes, the result is a quarter-note triplet:

one *uh* *and* *three* *uh* *and*

The notes must be *exactly* equal in length, with every two beats divided into three equal parts. (This can be difficult to hear at a slow tempo—once you know you're counting accurately, speed up a bit and the phrase will begin to sound more musical.) Don't confuse quarter-note triplets with another common phrase that is *not* a triplet (the notes are not all exactly equal in length):

Quarter-note triplets are often used to create rhythmic drama, particularly in a bluesy chord pattern like that shown here:

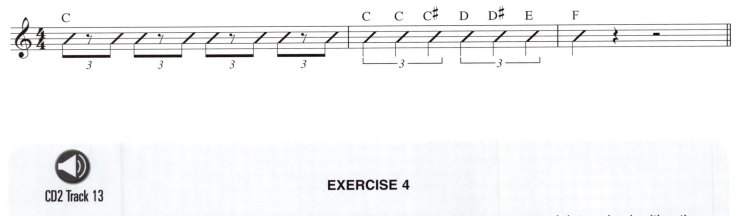

EXERCISE 4

CD2, Track 13 contains examples of eighth-, sixteenth-, and quarter-note triplets mixed with other rhythms. Use the same methods you've already learned (listen, sing, memorize, clap, write) to transcribe these rhythms.

CD2 Track 13

Triplet Feel

27

When triplet rhythms are used continuously throughout a piece of music, they are considered to be part of the basic "feel," or underlying rhythmic organization. Depending on tempo and style, triplet feels are typically described as either **compound meter** or **shuffle/swing**.

Compound Meter

When the rhythm of a piece of music is made up of steady eighth-note triplets over a pulse of 2, 3, or 4, rather than repetitiously writing "3" over every group of eighth notes, the triplets can be built into the time signature by using compound meter. Compound meter is created by taking a "simple" meter, such as 4/4, and multiplying the top number by three—reflecting the triplets—and representing the eighth notes by the bottom number, 8. The resulting time signature, **12/8**, designates a pulse of four beats per measure with three eighth notes per beat—exactly equivalent to 4/4 with triplets, but with a clearer expression of the overall rhythmic feel.

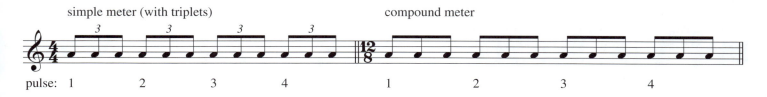

Another compound time signature is 6/8, equivalent to a meter of 2/4 with steady triplets (9/8—equivalent to a meter of 3/4 with steady triplets—is far less common than 12/8 or 6/8).

In popular music, compound meter is generally used only at slower tempos; when the tempo picks up, the triplet feeling is better defined as *shuffle* or *swing*.

Shuffle and Swing

Shuffle and swing are other versions of meter based on triplets. A **shuffle** is an eighth-note triplet with the middle note silent, notated either with a rest on the middle eighth note or with a quarter-note/eighth-note combination.

Swing is notated the same way, the only difference being in the interpretation. As a general rule, shuffles—closely associated with traditional blues—are played with the upbeat clearly articulated. Swing—typical of traditional jazz—shifts the emphasis onto the downbeat, with the upbeat played much more lightly.

Shuffle and swing feels are not reflected in the time signature, which remains simple (e.g., 4/4, 2/2, or 3/4). Instead, they are indicated by writing the word "shuffle" or "swing" above the staff at the beginning of the piece, which is understood to mean that ordinary eighth notes are to be played with a triplet feel. Sometimes notation is included to show the equivalence:

Triplet Feel and Diatonic Seventh Chord Progressions

Triplet feels (compound meter, shuffle, and swing) are heard in countless blues, jazz, pop, and R&B tunes, and diatonic seventh chords often provide the harmony for these styles as well. Transcription techniques for progressions combining these chords and rhythms are no different from the techniques we developed for triads combined with eighth- and sixteenth-note rhythms:

1. Identify the meter and key, and write the time and key signatures on the staff.
2. Sketch the rhythms below the staff.
3. Identify the bass line (root progression), and write chord symbols (letter name and quality) above the staff.
4. Transfer the rhythms onto the staff, lining up the chord symbols at the precise points where they occur.

CD2 Track 14

EXERCISE 1

CD2, Track 14 contains examples of progressions combining triplet feels and diatonic seventh chords. Transcribe them following the steps described above.

Blues

28

Blues has had such a major influence on popular music that its traces can be found in nearly every contemporary style. Combining African and European musical traditions, blues joins elements of the major and minor diatonic systems to produce a third system that is distinct from either one.

Dominant Tonality

In diatonic harmony, the function of the dominant seventh chord quality is to build a feeling of anticipation leading to a resolution; that is, V7 resolves to the major (I) or minor (Imi) tonic chord. This is also true for blues, but with an important difference—in blues, the tonic is also a dominant seventh chord, as is the IV chord. The relationship between the roots of I7, IV7, and V7 is the same as it is in diatonic progressions, but because the chords are *all* dominant sevenths, the progression never feels fully resolved in the traditional sense. This use of a dominant seventh quality as the tonic chord suggests a third tonality unlike either major or minor that can best be described as **dominant tonality**.

EXERCISE 1

Pick any comfortable note as a tonic, and sing dominant seventh arpeggios from the first, fourth, and fifth degrees of the scale.

When you return from the V7 arpeggio to the I7 arpeggio, the lowered seventh of the tonic chord prevents the harmony from feeling completely settled. This unresolved dissonance is part of what makes blues sound "bluesy."

Blues Form

Most blues progressions are made up of only three chords—I7, IV7, and V7—arranged in certain patterns that are traditionally learned and played by ear. The most common blues form by far is the **twelve-bar blues**. As the name implies, it is twelve bars in length, regardless of key or tempo, and it is traditionally performed with an eighth-note triplet shuffle rhythm. While there are several slight variations, the overall form is always essentially the same:

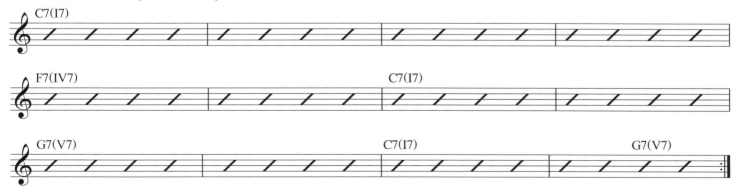

Other traditional blues progressions include eight-bar and sixteen-bar forms, each also with variations, but all based on the same three chords.

Blues Melody

Like the unusual harmonic structure of blues, blues melody is also different from either major or minor diatonic melody. Since blues harmony is based on the dominant seventh chord, neither the major nor minor scales exactly match the chord structure, so we need a new scale: the **dominant scale**. The dominant scale closely resembles a major scale, but with a lowered seventh degree.

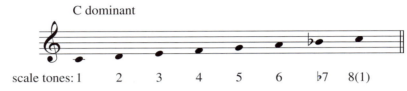

C dominant

scale tones: 1   2   3   4   5   6   ♭7   8(1)

EXERCISE 2

From any comfortable tonic, sing a one-octave major scale, and then lower the major seventh degree a half step to a minor seventh. Sing the scale with lowered seventh while playing a dominant seventh chord to hear the direct relationship between the scale and the chord. Sing the scale ascending and descending from various tonics until you can sing it accurately in both directions.

The dominant scale matches the quality of the dominant seventh chord, but it isn't inherently a "blues scale." The uniqueness of blues melody owes as much to the use of blues inflections as it does to the notes themselves. Two of these inflections are specific enough that they are called **blue notes**. The first blue note is the **minor third (♭3)** scale degree. Whether sustained or immediately resolved into the major third, against a dominant seventh chord the minor third creates a deliberate dissonance that has come to be described simply as "bluesy."

EXERCISE 3

On a guitar or piano, play a dominant seventh chord, and sing the following melodic phrases:

1	**♭3**	**1**	
1	**♭3**	**3**	
1	**♭3**	**3**	**1**
1	**♭3**	**3**	**5**

The true blue note inflection actually sits *between* the minor and major thirds. To hear it, sing the minor third and let your voice slide gradually upward toward the major third, without quite reaching it. To achieve this effect on the guitar, you bend the string slightly; on a piano, you can only approximate by playing the minor and major thirds simultaneously or rolling quickly from one into the other, a typical blues piano phrasing technique.

The second blue note, usually called the **"flat five" (♭5)**, is the note a half step below the perfect fifth.

EXERCISE 4

On a guitar or piano, play a dominant seventh chord, and sing the following melodic phrases:

1	**♭3**	**5**	**♭5**	**5**	
1	**♭3**	**4**	**♭5**	**5**	
5	**♭5**	**4**	**♭3**	**3**	**1**

Chapter 28

Pentatonic Scales

The dominant scale combined with blue notes provides all of the notes typically used in blues melodies, but because it contains so many notes, it is too complex to be practical for ear training purposes. Contained within it, however, are two smaller scales, the major pentatonic and the minor pentatonic. By definition, pentatonic scales contain just five notes, making them more realistic to hear and play, and each of these scales contains the raw material for a great number of blues phrases.

The **major pentatonic** scale contains the tonic, major second, major third, perfect fifth, and major sixth, a set of notes that emphasizes the sweeter melodic qualities of the larger dominant scale.

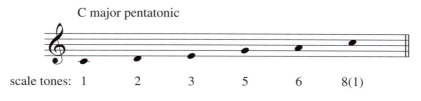

C major pentatonic

scale tones: 1   2   3   5   6   8(1)

EXERCISE 5

From any comfortable tonic, sing a one-octave dominant scale using scale step numbers. Sing the scale again, this time singing the major pentatonic scale tones out loud and the other tones silently:

1   **2**   **3**   4   **5**   **6**   ♭7   **8**

Finally, sing just the major pentatonic tones ascending and descending. Repeat from different tonics until you can sing the major pentatonic scale without filling in the extra major scale tones.

The **minor pentatonic** scale contains the tonic, perfect fourth, perfect fifth, and minor seventh, plus a blue note—the minor third. As such, it's darker and more dissonant than the major pentatonic. (Adding the second blue note to the minor pentatonic—the flat five—creates what is commonly called the "**blues scale**.")

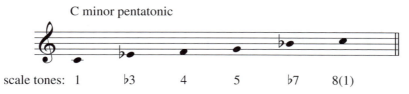

C minor pentatonic

scale tones: 1   ♭3   4   5   ♭7   8(1)

EXERCISE 6

From any comfortable tonic, sing a one-octave dominant scale using scale step numbers. Next, sing the minor pentatonic scale tones out loud and the other notes silently:

1   2   **♭3**   3   **4**   **5**   6   **♭7**   **8**

Finally, sing just the minor pentatonic scale tones ascending and descending. Repeat from other tonics until you can sing the minor pentatonic accurately without using the extra tones for reference.

With these different combinations of notes and inflections, blues musicians can choose among a great variety of emotional shadings, and melodies rarely conform exclusively to a single, particular scale.

EXERCISE 7

Listen to **CD2**, **Track 15**, and transcribe each example—melody and chords—following these steps:

1. Determine the meter and key, and write the time signature and key signature on the staff. As a rule, blues melody and harmony is notated using the major key signature of the tonic chord with the "blue notes" indicated by accidentals.

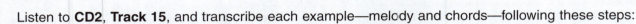

2. Transcribe the melodic rhythm and sketch it below the staff. Usually in blues, the eighth notes are shuffled; indicate this by simply writing "shuffle" above the staff.

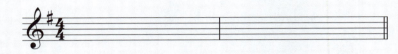

3. Transcribe the notes on the staff. In blues phrasing, it's very common to hear two notes—particularly the minor and major thirds—played nearly simultaneously. In this case, the first note is often written as a **grace note**—that is, an embellishment without a precise rhythmic value—connected to the second note by a slur (a curved line that shows a smooth connection between two different pitches).

4. Add the rhythmic values to the notes, and erase the sketch:

5. Using the techniques you've already learned for transcribing chords, write the chord symbols above the staff. Since the melody is already on the staff, there is no need for specific rhythmic notation—whatever beat or part of a beat a chord occurs on, write the chord symbol directly above it:

Now that the example is notated, visualize how you will play the melody on your instrument—where your hands will be and what fingering you'll use—then actually play it. If you have visualized properly, the melody will fall under your fingers and you will play it correctly the first time. Using the same method, visualize and play the chords. Visualization is an important bridge between ear training as a concept and its application to your playing, and exact visualization has the reverse effect of improving your ability to transcribe by helping you to "see" the music as you write it down.

Part IV
Combinations and Variations

The first three parts of this book have covered most of the standard patterns of melody, harmony, and rhythm used in popular music. In this final part, you'll learn combinations and variations of these basic ingredients that produce some of the more complex but still common sounds you hear every day.

You'll also see how the basic skills of pitch matching, analytical listening, and pattern recognition enable you to identify almost any new sound, even when diatonic rules are being stretched or broken.

Modal Interchange
29

In the previous section, you learned how blues borrows elements of major and minor systems to create a hybrid. This mixture of diatonic systems is not limited to blues, however—it's a fundamental feature of all styles of popular music.

Mixing Diatonic Systems

Play the following chord progression on a guitar or keyboard:

Which chord is the tonic? Your ear will tell you it's the A major triad, but according to the rules of the major diatonic system, the rest of the progression doesn't make any sense—the G and C triads do not belong to the A major scale harmony. Both G and C *can* be found in the A minor scale harmony, but then the A major chord itself doesn't fit in. How, then, can these three chords sound so natural together if they don't obey the rules of diatonic harmony? The answer is found in a concept called **modal interchange**.

Simply put, modal interchange is the mixing of **parallel** major and minor diatonic systems. Parallel systems are those built from the same tonic, e.g., A major and A minor. In traditional musical terminology, the major and minor diatonic systems are called "modes," and modal interchange involves interchanging, or mixing, chords from one system with those from the parallel system (the concept applies to both triads and seventh chord harmonies).

Major	I	IImi	IIImi	IV	V	VImi	VII°
A major	A	Bmi	C#mi	D	E	F#mi	G#°
A minor	Ami	B°	C	Dmi	Emi	F	G
Minor	**Imi**	**II°**	**♭III**	**IVmi**	**Vmi**	**♭VI**	**♭VII**

EXERCISE 1

Play the three major triads that belong to the A major harmonized scale (I, IV, and V):

A   D   E

Play the three major triads that belong to the A minor harmonized scale (♭III, ♭VI, ♭VII):

C   F   G

Play all six triads in a row, mixing the two chord sets:

A   C   D   E   F   G   A

When played in a row from A to A, they all clearly fit together regardless of which system they originated from. What holds these chords together is that, despite their different origins, they are all related to the same tonic note. With this concept in mind, it becomes clear why the first progression (A–G–C–A) "works"—the A chord is the tonic of the A major tonality, and the G and C chords are "borrowed" from the parallel minor tonality, A minor.

Literally thousands of tunes that blur the rules of distinct major and minor tonalities can be understood through the concept of modal interchange. Like blues, the explanation is more complicated than the results, and with some transcribing experience you are likely to start "hearing" modal interchange quicker than you can describe it.

Chapter 29

Transcribing Modal Interchange Progressions

Once the major and minor systems are combined, the number of mathematically possible combinations of bass line and chord quality in a single key seems enormous. Fortunately, in practice, a relatively small number of progressions are used again and again. Although modal interchange more often involves a major tonality borrowing from its parallel minor, it works both ways. In either case:

1. Begin by listening to the whole progression and identifying the quality of the tonic chord (major or minor).

2. As you analyze the progression, compare the bass notes to the diatonic scale of the tonic chord. If a note doesn't fit, compare it to the parallel scale (in the following exercise, it's a certainty that it will belong to one or the other).

3. Listen carefully to the quality of each chord. Strictly diatonic rules no longer apply—in some cases, modal interchange involves chords built on the same bass note but with different qualities, such as IV major and IV minor.

Compared to diatonic progressions, modal interchange introduces a new twist—bass notes and chord qualities are no longer automatically linked. But the techniques you've learned for identifying bass lines and qualities in diatonic progressions still work, and the following exercise will provide you with some experience.

CD2 Track 16

EXERCISE 2

CD2, Track 16 contains chord progressions with modal interchange. Listen and follow these steps as you transcribe each example:

1. Identify the meter and tonality, and write the time and key signatures on the staff (use either a major or minor key signature depending on the quality of the tonic chord):

2. Identify the rhythms and write them on the staff using rhythmic notation:

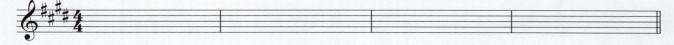

3. Identify the bass line and write the letter name of each bass note above the staff in its proper location above the rhythm:

4. Identify the quality of each chord, and add it to the letter name. If in doubt about the quality, use the "pitch freezing" method—pause the CD as soon as you hear the chord, and match pitch with the chord tones.

Secondary Dominants
30

Modal interchange explains how major and minor diatonic systems are routinely mixed, adding to the number of chord possibilities within each tonality. Another way in which diatonic systems are stretched is by using the dominant seventh chord outside of its primary function as the V7 chord of a given key. Dominant chords used in this way are called **secondary dominants**.

EXERCISE 1

Play this chord progression on a guitar or keyboard:

Now play this progression—notice the change from Ami to A7:

Sing the root and third of each chord in the first progression:

Now sing the root and third of each chord in the second progression

When you play and sing the two progressions back-to-back, the difference is subtle but distinct—the A7 chord moves to D minor with more energy than A minor, as the major third (C♯) resolves upward to the root of D minor with more energy than the minor third (C natural). Like all dominant seventh chords, A7 has a built-in dissonance, an "inner urge" to resolve to the next chord, that is at the heart of the primary V7-I resolution, but in this progression A7 is not the V7 chord of the key and D minor is not the tonic; they are the VI and II chords, respectively. Therefore, A7 is labeled "V7 of II" ("five seven of two," or simply "five of two"); it is a *secondary* dominant.

The explanation above tells why secondary dominants work, but where are they used, and how can you identify them? In answer to the first question, secondary dominants fall into two main categories: **functioning** (i.e., resolving up a perfect fourth or down a perfect fifth into the next chord, as A7 resolves to Dmi) and **non-functioning** (i.e., *not* resolving up a fourth or down a fifth into the next chord).

Chapter 30

Functioning Secondary Dominants

Functioning secondary dominants are used when a composer wants to inject a greater feeling of movement into a diatonic progression, as in the previous example. In theory, any chord—triad or seventh—in the diatonic major or minor harmonized scale that resolves up a fourth/down a fifth can be altered to make it a secondary dominant:

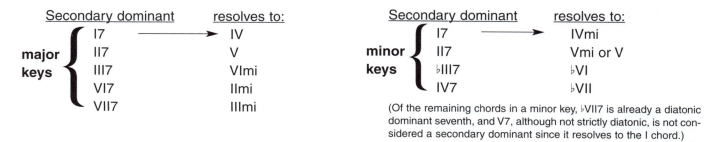

A secondary dominant may also resolve into another secondary dominant. Go back to the progression in Exercise 1 and change D minor to D7. Listen to the result as it resolves into G7:

Each dominant chord resolves into the next, and the progression does not fully resolve until it finally returns to the tonic chord. The bass line is diatonic but the chord qualities are not; careful attention to quality is vital.

EXERCISE 2

CD2 Track 17

CD2, Track 17 contains chord progressions featuring secondary dominants. Listen and transcribe each example, as you follow these steps (use Roman numerals to identify the chords):

1. Listen to the progression; learn and sing the bass line:

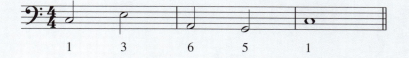

2. Listen for chord quality. Secondary dominants have a greater feeling of "urgency" than diatonic triads and seventh chords. If a diatonic minor chord is altered to become a secondary dominant, the third is raised; for a diatonic major chord, the seventh is lowered. Use the pitch freezing technique as needed.

Functioning secondary dominants are explained in theory as "five of something," e.g. V7/II ("five seven of two"), but it is most practical to hear them and number them as alterations of diatonic chords. In the example shown above, the E7 chord may be explained as "V7/VI," but it is numbered simply as III7—identify the root, identify the quality, and name the chord accordingly.

Non-Functioning Secondary Dominants: "Bluesy" Harmony

Dominant seventh chords may also be substituted for diatonic chords that do not resolve up a fourth/down a fifth and may even be used in place of other, non-diatonic chords. This leads to a very wide range of possible applications and explanations, but regardless of theory, any chord progression is ultimately the sum of two parts: bass line and chord quality.

Since dominant chords form the basis of blues harmony, it's often helpful to think of secondary dominants—functioning and non-functioning—as adding a "bluesy" character to a progression, and many composers use them for just this effect. Secondary dominants are a staple of jazz and R&B progressions where the blues element is always at least suggested if not boldly stated. The greater your familiarity with blues and blues-related styles, the easier you will find it to recognize this distinctive stylistic quality wherever you hear it.

In Chapter 36, which summarizes the method for hearing various types of non-diatonic (chromatic) harmony, you'll find examples of secondary dominants in typical combinations with other chords. Regardless of the complexity, the steps for identifying any progression remain the same:

1. Identify the bass line in relation to the tonality.
2. Identify each chord's quality in relation to its root.

The more tunes you become familiar with and learn to play, the more you will begin to hear chord progressions as complete patterns rather than individual, isolated sounds.

Inverted Chords

31

Up to this point, we've taken for granted the idea that chords are always built with the root in the bass—find the lowest note, and you've found the name of the chord. While in practice this is true most of the time, chords can also be built with any chord tone—third, fifth, or seventh—in the bass. Chords rearranged in this way are called **inverted chords**, or simply **inversions**. By expanding the number of available bass notes, inversions create additional options for bass lines within diatonic chord progressions without affecting either chord function or quality.

Triads

Triads contain three notes; voicing the root in the bass—called "root position"—is not considered an inversion, so there are two possible inversions of any triad. In traditional terminology, a chord with the third in the bass is said to be in *first inversion*. A chord with the fifth in the bass is in *second inversion*.

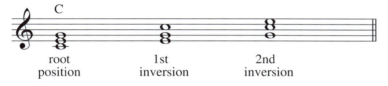

root position   1st inversion   2nd inversion

The first step in learning to recognize these inversions is to sing consonant triad voicings from notes other than the root.

EXERCISE 1

Sing major triads with notes ascending in the following order (continue past the octave in the second and third examples (3=10, 5=12):

1	3	5	8
3	5	8	3(10)
5	8	3(10)	5(12)

Repeat the same exercise with minor triads.

EXERCISE 2

CD2 Track 18

Listen to **CD2**, **Track 18**, and identify the major and minor triad inversions, following these steps:

1. Sing the lowest note, followed by the other notes in any order you hear them.
2. Identify which note is the root by singing the notes in different combinations, trying different tones on the bottom of the chord until the notes line up in a familiar 1-3-5 arpeggio. (Exercise 1, singing inverted arpeggios, is the best preparation for this step.)
3. When you've found the root, identify the note in the bass (third or fifth) and name the inversion.
4. Identify the quality.

Seventh Chords

Seventh chords contain four notes, so there are three possible inversions of each seventh chord. In traditional terminology, a chord with the seventh in the bass is called *third inversion*.

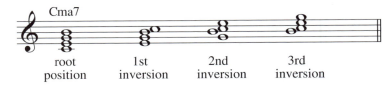

root
position   1st
inversion   2nd
inversion   3rd
inversion

The method for singing, analyzing, and identifying inverted seventh chords is the same as that for triads.

EXERCISE 3

Sing major seventh arpeggios with notes ascending in the following order (in order to reach the highest note, start on a note that's low in your vocal range):

1	3	5	7	8
3	5	7	8	3
5	7	8	3	5
7	8	3	5	7

Repeat the same exercise with dominant sevenths and minor sevenths (inverted minor seven flat-five chords are considerably rarer in practice).

CD2 Track 19

EXERCISE 4

Identify the inverted major, minor, and dominant seventh chords on **CD2**, **Track 19** using the same techniques you used for Exercise 2.

Naming Inverted Chords

In order to notate inversions, a different type of chord symbol is used: the **slash chord.** Slash chords contain two letter names separated by a diagonal line, or slash. The letter on the left indicates the name and quality of the chord, and the letter on the right indicates the name of the bass note:

chord

C/E   Cmi/E♭   Cma7/G   C7/B♭

bass note

(When slash chords are described in words, the slash is indicated by the word "over," as in "C *over* E.")

Chapter 31

CD2 Tracks 18 & 19

EXERCISE 5

Name the inversions from Exercises 2 and 4 using slash chords symbols—just add the appropriate chord quality and bass note to each root indicated below:

Ex. 2
1. F   2. F   3. F   4. E   5. C#   6. F#   7. E♭   8. E   9. B   10. A

Ex. 4
1. G   2. D   3. B♭   4. C   5. F   6. G   7. G   8. A   9. D   10. A♭

Play each chord on your instrument and compare it to the recorded example to see if they sound the same. Since the slash chord symbol only tells a player which note to play in the bass but gives no information on how to voice the rest of the notes, voicings of the same inversion and chord quality may differ.

NOTE: On the guitar, inverted chords are often tricky to finger. If you don't know how to play inverted chord voicings, match the recording by playing the chord in root position using any voicing you know, then play the inverted bass note separately. If you've identified the quality correctly, the two sounds will add up to a match.

Inverted Chords in Progressions

Once you've gained some skill at singing and identifying inverted chords one at a time, the next step is to recognize them in progressions. In theory, any chord can be inverted, but in popular practice the most commonly inverted chords are I, IV, and V, so we'll limit our examples initially to those three chords. Also, while there would appear to be a mind-boggling number of possibilities for using inverted chords in progressions, in fact only a few combinations are used over and over. This means that identifying inverted chords in their normal musical setting is easier than identifying individual, unrelated voicings.

NOTE: Inverted chords may also be represented by numbers. Use a Roman numeral with chord quality on the left side of the slash instead of the chord's letter name, and put the Arabic number representing the chord tone of the bass note on the right (3=major third, ♭3=minor third, ♭7=minor seventh, etc.—make sure the quality of the bass note matches the quality of the chord itself).

CD2 Track 20

EXERCISE 6

CD2, Track 20 contains major and minor progressions with inverted chords (mostly I, IV, and V, but other chords are also inverted). Listen to each example, and transcribe it following these steps:

1. Listen to the progression, learn and sing the bass line

2. Identify known, root-position chords first.

3. When you hear an unfamiliar chord:
   a. sing the chord tones in any order you hear them.
   b. identify the root (as in Exercises 2 and 4).
   c. identify the degree of the lowest note (3rd, 5th, or 7th).

4. Name the chord using a slash chord symbol.

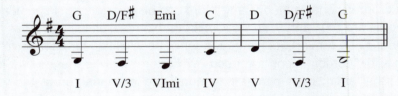

5. Play the progression on your instrument, and compare it to the track. (Guitarists recall the note in Exercise 5 about playing inverted chords.)

32 Triads with Added Tones

Major triads, minor triads, and power chords are simple, uncluttered sounds, which makes them at the same time both appealing and predictable. Over the years, writers and players have devised ways to add color to triad-based harmonies without making them too complex. This is done by adding notes outside the basic 1-3-5 structure—in particular, the **major second**, the **perfect fourth**, and the **major sixth**.

The Major Second

The major second creates a softly dissonant, "shimmering" effect when added to a triad or power chord voicing (as a rule, added tones are placed in the upper part of a chord, both to highlight the effect and to avoid muddiness). This effect isn't apparent when you sing the tones separately—it only appears when the chord is played as a whole.

EXERCISE 1

On a guitar or a keyboard, play the following chord voicings, sustaining the chord while you sing the added second (you can sing in any octave that's comfortable):

There are three chord symbols that describe triads or power chords with added seconds, regardless of what octave or in what order the notes are voiced (being relatively recent sounds in popular music, consistent chord symbols have not yet evolved, but these names are logical and widely used):

5/2: a power chord with an added second degree (e.g., C5/2)
2: a major triad with an added second degree (e.g., C2)
mi2: a minor triad with an added second degree (e.g., Cmi2)

The Perfect Fourth

The fourth is nearly always added in place of, rather than alongside, the third in a major or minor triad, resulting in a **suspended**, **sus4**, or simply **sus** chord (e.g., Csus). As the name implies, the fourth is suspended above the third, creating a feeling of tension that is relieved when the note resolves down to the third.

EXERCISE 2

Play the following chord voicings sustaining the notes while you sing the fourths and thirds (sing in any octave that's comfortable):

32

In the examples you just sang, the F of the Csus chord resolves to E (the major third of C) or E♭ (the minor third). In traditional musical practice, the fourth always resolves to the third, but in popular music the sus chord is sometimes left unresolved to capitalize on its effect of anticipation.

The Major Sixth

Adding the major sixth to a major triad adds sweetness; adding it to a minor triad has a more dissonant effect.

EXERCISE 3

Sing the arpeggios and then play them, sustaining the notes so they all sound together:

NOTE: It is difficult to sustain these notes on a guitar—to get a similar effect, play a major or minor triad and sing the major sixth against it.

The chord symbols are:

6: a major triad with an added sixth (e.g., C6)
mi6: a minor triad with an added sixth (e.g., Gmi6)

It is also common to add both the major sixth and the major second to a triad. When both are combined in a single chord, tradition dictates that the second is called a ninth (an octave plus a step):

6/9: a major triad with added sixth and ninth (e.g., F♯6/9)
mi6/9: a minor triad with added sixth and ninth (e.g., B♭mi6/9)

Identifying Chords with Added Tones

If you've practiced the information in this book up to now, you've already gained considerable experience at identifying major and minor triads, and power chords. Each of these new chords (2, sus, 6, 6/9, etc.) has a distinct sound, but all are based on those qualities. To name them, first identify the underlying quality and then concentrate on the added color. With experience, you'll begin to hear the chord as a whole.

EXERCISE 4

CD2 Track 21

Listen to **CD2, Track 21** and identify the chord types by following these steps:

1. Locate the root (always the bottom note in these examples), then the third, identifying the quality. If there is no third, it's a power chord variation or a sus chord.
2. Listen for the non-chord tone (i.e., any note that isn't 1, 3, or 5), sing it, and compare it to the root. What's the interval? Combining the added note to the basic quality, what is the name of the chord?

When you've identified each chord and its added tone, create the chord symbol, adding the appropriate quality to the corresponding root below. Finally, visualize and play each chord on your instrument (sing the added tone, where necessary), and compare it to the track.

1. F_____ 2. B♭_____ 3. E_____ 4. B_____ 5. B_____ 6. G_____ 7. F_____ 8. A♭_____

Extended Chords

33

When major second, perfect fourth, and major sixth intervals are added to seventh chords, the added tones are called **extensions**, and the chords themselves are called **extended chords.** Extended chords are especially common in jazz harmony, where triad-based chords are considered too plain.

Ninth Chords

Adding a major second to a seventh chord results in a ninth chord (extended chords are named by their highest extension). There are three common ninth chord qualities:

Quality	Structure	Symbol
major ninth	major seventh chord + major second	**ma9** (e.g., Cma9)
minor ninth	minor seventh chord + major second	**mi9** (e.g., Cmi9)
dominant ninth	dominant seventh chord + major second	**9** (e.g., C9)

In theory, a ninth may be added to the minor seven flat-five chord, but this chord is rare in popular music.

EXERCISE 1

Play the arpeggio of each seventh chord quality, and sing the ninth in any comfortable octave:

Eleventh Chords

Adding a perfect fourth interval to major, minor, and dominant ninth chords would logically seem to result in three qualities of eleventh chords, but common practice is different. In dominant seventh or ninth chords, the fourth replaces the third, resulting in a sus chord (often called an eleventh chord, although technically it isn't). Major seventh or major ninth chords containing a fourth are rare, with or without the third. This means that the only "true" eleventh chord in common use is the minor eleventh.

Quality	Structure	Symbol
(7,9) sus	minor or dominant seventh/ninth chord with the fourth replacing the third	**7sus, 9sus*** (e.g., C7sus)
minor 11th	minor seventh/ninth chord with an added fourth	**mi11** (e.g., Cmi11)

*9sus chords are also commonly notated as slash chords, for example, C9sus = B♭/C (B♭ major triad voiced over a C bass note). The slash chord name is simpler to visualize and play and is an equally accurate way to symbolize the sound.

EXERCISE 2

On a guitar or keyboard, play the following chords, sustaining the notes while you sing the fourth/ eleventh (in any comfortable octave):

Thirteenth Chords

Adding a major sixth interval to a major, minor, or dominant seventh or ninth chord creates a thirteenth chord (in theory, thirteenth chords may contain an eleventh, but in practice they rarely do).

Quality	Structure	Symbol
major 13th	major seventh or ninth chord + major sixth	**ma13** (e.g., Cma13)
minor 13th	minor seventh or ninth chord + major sixth	**mi13** (e.g., Cmi13)
dominant 13th	dominant seventh or ninth chord + major sixth	**13** (e.g., C13)

EXERCISE 3

On a guitar or keyboard, play the arpeggios, sustaining the notes as you sing the thirteenth:

Identifying Extended Chords

Identifying extended chords is a two-part process: first, identify the underlying seventh chord quality, and then identify any extensions.

EXERCISE 4

CD2 Track 22

Listen to **CD2**, **Track 22** and identify the extended chords by following these steps:

1. Identify the root.
2. Match pitch with the third, then with the seventh. This combination will tell you the underlying seventh chord quality:

> Major third + major seventh = major seventh chord
> Major third + minor seventh = dominant seventh chord
> Minor third + minor seventh = minor seventh chord

3. Match pitch with any note that sounds like it's outside the basic structure, then compare to the root to determine its interval quality (extensions are usually voiced at or near the top of the chord). The combination of the underlying seventh chord quality plus the additional interval(s) gives you the name of the extended chord.

Once you've identified each chord, create the chord symbol by adding the appropriate quality to the corresponding root below. Visualize and play the chords (sing the extensions, if necessary) on your instrument.

1. E   2. D   3. D   4. B♭   5. F   6. B♭   7. A   8. C   9. D   10. C♯

____   ____   ____   ____   ____   ____   ____   ____   ____   ____

Extensions enrich the sound of chords, but they do not change the quality or function, so practically speaking, being able to identify the underlying quality of a chord is more important than being able to identify specific extensions. Like the basic diatonic chord qualities, extended chords have unique personalities, and the more you play these chords on your instrument, the more familiar they become. In the end, playing experience is a very important factor in developing a great ear.

Diatonic Melodies with Chromatic Tones

34

Diatonic melodies are very common in popular music, but so are melodies that include notes outside of the diatonic scales—i.e., **chromatic tones**. Blues is a prime example of a style that routinely includes notes outside of a major or minor tonality. In this chapter, we'll look at other types of non-diatonic, or chromatic, melodies.

Chromatic Tones

Diatonic scales contain seven tones—that leaves five non-scale tones, a.k.a., chromatic notes, within any given octave. (The chromatic scale, which consists of all twelve half steps, is not in itself a practical source of melodies in popular music because it lacks a clear tonality.)

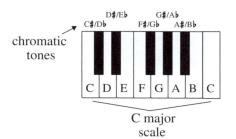

Our perception of the melodic dissonance created by chromatic tones is a result of the degree of rhythmic or dynamic stress given to these notes against the background harmony. Depending on the amount of emphasis placed on a chromatic tone, it can be nearly unnoticeable or strikingly dissonant.

EXERCISE 1

1. Sing the following melody at a medium tempo while playing a C major triad on your instrument.

2. At the same tempo, sing the following melody with chromatic tones:

In the second melody, D♯ increases the pull toward E while E♭ falls away toward D. The emphasis remains on the tonic and major third, so the effect of the chromatic tones is to create a denser melodic line, but not dissonance.

3. Now sing the line again while playing the C major triad, and hang onto the E♭:

In this example, placing a strong rhythmic accent on the E♭ creates tension between the minor third in the melody and the major third in the triad. Here, the use of a chromatic tone results in greater dissonance.

EXERCISE 2

1. Sing a major triad arpeggio:

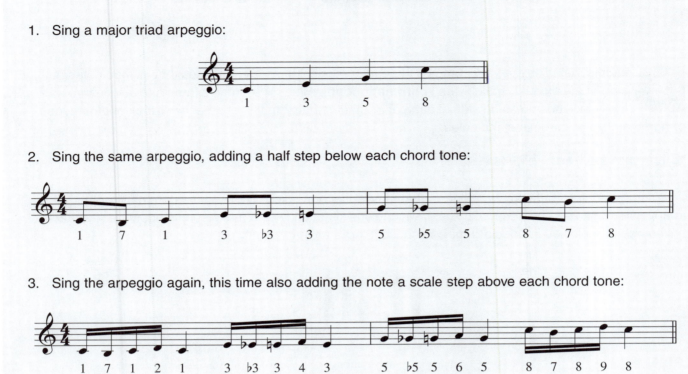

2. Sing the same arpeggio, adding a half step below each chord tone:

3. Sing the arpeggio again, this time also adding the note a scale step above each chord tone:

4. Repeat the exercise with a minor triad.

Chromatic tones used within an overall diatonic context are generally given labels such as **passing tones** (as in Exercise 1) or **neighboring tones** (as in Exercise 2). These names reflect the way we hear chromatic tones weaving through or hovering around the otherwise diatonic structure.

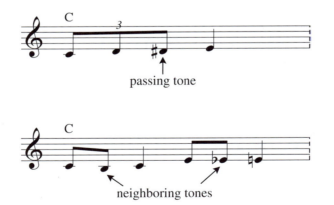

passing tone

neighboring tones

To transcribe melodies with chromatic tones accurately, we depend upon precise pitch matching as well as constant comparison between chromatic phrases and the scales around which they are built.

Chapter 34

EXERCISE 3

Listen to **CD2**, **Track 23**, and transcribe each melody on the staff, following these steps.

1. Locate and identify the tonic and the tonality (major or minor).
2. From the tonic, sing the scale that best matches the tonality.

3. Write the key and time signatures, and sketch the melodic rhythm below the staff. Identify the familiar-sounding notes first (e.g., chord tones, diatonic scale tones), and pencil them in on the staff.

4. Focus on the "in-between" notes, and identify them by comparing them to the diatonic scale.
5. Write the melody (including rhythm) on the staff, indicating the chromatic tones with accidentals.

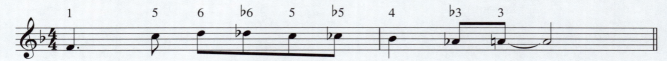

6. Visualize the melody on your instrument.
7. Play the melody, and compare it to the original.

When chromatic variations are used consistently throughout a piece of music, they may represent scales other than major, minor, or dominant. Just naming these scales, let alone learning each of their unique sounds, is a considerable task, but is not a requirement for ear training. (Another category of chromatic melodies, those based on non-diatonic harmonies, will be covered in Chapter 37.) Whether a raised seventh degree in a minor melody represents a passing tone in natural minor or the presence of the harmonic minor scale, for example, is more a problem for theoreticians than for listeners. With the tools you've already developed, you have the means to identify any non-diatonic melody by comparing it to the underlying major, minor, or dominant tonality; the rest is mainly a matter of listening and playing experience.

35 Non-Diatonic Chord Qualities

Most of the chords in popular music are diatonic triads, seventh chords, or variations and extensions of these qualities, but a few other unique chord types occur often enough to deserve special attention.

The Diminished Seventh Chord

The diminished triad was introduced as part of the harmonized major and minor scales (VII° and II°, respectively). Adding a diminished seventh interval to this triad creates a diminished seventh chord.

EXERCISE 1

Compare the diminished seventh chord structure to other seventh chords by singing the following arpeggios in order:

Major seventh	1	3	5	7	8
Dominant seventh	1	3	5	♭7	8
Minor seventh	1	♭3	5	♭7	8
Minor seven flat-five	1	♭3	♭5	♭7	8
Diminished seventh	1	♭3	♭5	♭♭7	8

The diminished seventh ("double flat seventh") interval of the diminished arpeggio is one half step lower than the minor seventh of the minor seven flat-five arpeggio (both are based on a diminished triad). This results in a very unusual chord structure: Every note in the diminished seventh chord is the same number of steps from the notes on either side of it. Because of this symmetry, the diminished chord structure sounds the same no matter how the chord is inverted, so any of its four chord tones can act as the root. Its uniquely ambiguous structure and distinct sound set the diminished seventh chord apart from other seventh chord qualities wherever it occurs.

EXERCISE 2

On a guitar or keyboard, play the following progressions:

In the first progression, the diminished chord replaces the diatonic VII chord in the key. In the second progression, the #IV°7 connects the diatonic IV chord to the diatonic I chord, a function generally known as a **passing chord** (the harmonic equivalent of a "passing note" in the melody). Although the diminished seventh chord takes on different guises due to its structure, these two roles—substituting for the V chord and acting as a passing chord—summarize its uses. In both cases, it acts as the "glue" between two more identifiable diatonic chords.

The Minor/Major Seventh Chord

Adding a major seventh interval to a minor triad results in a unique seventh chord quality with a common but very specific application.

The minor/major seventh chord is almost never heard on its own—it's nearly always sandwiched between the minor triad and the minor seventh chord in a distinctive harmonic pattern that has been used in dozens of popular songs from "Michelle" and "Something" by the Beatles to "Stairway to Heaven" by Led Zeppelin and "My Funny Valentine" by Rodgers and Hart. Exercise 3 illustrates the pattern.

EXERCISE 3

Sing and play the following arpeggios in order from the same root:

	1	♭3	5	8
minor	1	♭3	5	8
minor (major 7)	1	♭3	5	7
minor 7	1	♭3	5	♭7
minor 6	1	♭3	5	6

The Augmented Triad

The augmented triad is one of the four unique triad qualities, alongside major, minor, and diminished. Augmented triads contain a root, major third, and **augmented** (raised) **fifth**. The chord symbol for an augmented triad is "+," as in C+.

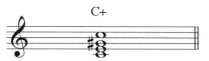

EXERCISE 4

1. Sing a major triad arpeggio ascending (1-3-5).
2. From the perfect fifth, sing up a half step to the augmented fifth.
3. Sing the root, major third, and augmented fifth in succession (1-3-♯5).
4. Add the octave to make a four-note arpeggio (1-3-♯5-8).
5. Repeat the exercise from another root.

The augmented triad may be tricky to sing at first, but its distinctive quality also makes it memorable. In practice, it is generally used in place of a major triad to create a sense of increased anticipation for the following chord, as illustrated in the following exercise.

EXERCISE 5

Sing and play the following chords in order, voicing the chord tones from each root as written:

In the example above, the G+ replaces the normal G major triad as the V chord, creating a greater feeling of tension before the resolution to C major. Now try this:

In this example, the C+ is a passing chord between C and C6, again raising the tension before resolving to the IV chord, F.

Altered Chords

Each of the three chords already described—diminished seventh, minor/major seventh, and augmented triad—is a non-diatonic chord quality with common applications in popular music. Another, broader category of non-diatonic chords is called **altered chords**; that is, diatonic chords in which one or more chord tones have been altered without affecting the underlying quality. In simplest terms (putting **enharmonics** aside—tones with the same pitch but different names, such as C♯ and D♭), alterations involve raising or lowering the fifth or the ninth chord degrees. Alterations create dissonance; so most altered chords are used as functioning dominant-quality chords, i.e., dominant chords that resolve to a tonic (as V7 resolves to I).

Like chromatic melodic tones, dominant chord alterations can be most easily heard within a diatonic structure, with certain alterations and resolutions occurring more frequently than others.

EXERCISE 6

Play the chords as you sing the melodic line:

In each case, the altered tone on the V7 chord resolves either up or down a half step into a tonic chord tone.

Identifying Non-Diatonic Chord Qualities

Each of the chord types discussed in this chapter has certain specific applications within a diatonic framework, which generally involve resolving directly to a diatonic chord. As a result, it is often easiest to identify these chords by transcribing the diatonic chords around them first; in particular, identify the chord of resolution, then work backward to the non-diatonic chord, identifying its quality first and alterations next.

CD2 Track 24

EXERCISE 7

Listen to **CD2**, **Track 24** and transcribe each progression as you follow these steps:

1. Transcribe the bass line:

2. Fill in the known diatonic chord qualities:

3. The dominant chord contains an alteration. Listen to the V-I progression to identify the chromatic resolution, i.e., identify which tone of the tonic chord is approached by a chromatic tone from which direction.

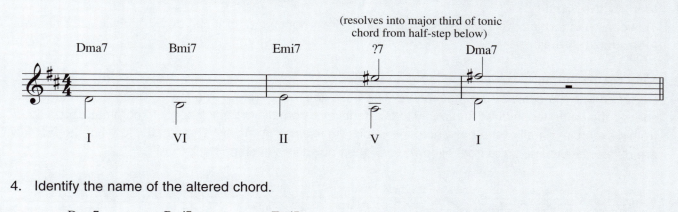

4. Identify the name of the altered chord.

Chromatic Progressions
36

Popular music harmony is built on the foundation of the diatonic major and minor systems, but most progressions contain some combination of chord functions or structures that are chromatic (i.e., non-diatonic). Examples of chromatic harmony include blues, modal interchange, and secondary dominants, as well as individual chords like the diminished seventh, minor/major seventh, augmented, and altered. Music theory provides a conceptual framework for explaining how chromatic harmony works, but to the listener/transcriber, the explanation for why a certain chord is used becomes relevant only after the chord has already been heard and correctly identified.

Fortunately, chromatic harmony in popular music is generally used within restricted limits—if the harmony is too dissonant, after all, it's not likely to be popular. With the ear training fundamentals we've already covered, you are equipped to identify any typical combination of bass line and quality; all that you need is experience. After you've analyzed a few progressions by ear, studying the theory behind them in greater detail will help you to narrow the range of likely choices the next time you are confronted with something unusual.

Transcribing Chromatic Harmony

Any combination of chord functions and qualities may be accurately transcribed by following a few logical steps.

CD2 Track 25

EXERCISE 1

Listen to **CD2**, **Track 25**, as you apply these steps to transcribe typical chromatic progressions.

1. **Identify the tonality.**
   This can be in terms of relative pitch (e.g., major, minor, dominant), or it can be by specific letter name—for example, A major.

2. **Sing the bass line.**
   Compare it to the scale of the tonic chord. The bass line, although it's in a low register, is still a melodic line, so the same techniques that apply to transcribing chromatic melodies apply to chromatic bass lines. In this example, do all of the bass notes fit within the scale of A major? The first five do, but the last few are different—the line goes from E down to C, then down in half steps back to A:

104

3. Identify the chord qualities.

Notate each chord including name (or number) and quality. Keep in mind that the bass line may include chord inversions—not every bass note is necessarily a root.

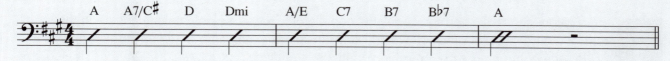

Chord quality is determined by comparing each chord structure to its root, not to the underlying tonality. Again, avoid making assumptions about quality without checking the actual structure. Stop the recording as soon as the unknown chord is played; sing the root, then let your voice intuitively match pitch with the sound of the third as it lingers in your memory. Analyze the interval—major or minor—then play the segment again to double-check for accuracy. Repeat the process for the fifth and added tones, seventh, extensions, and/or alterations, if present.

4. Visualize and play the results.

After you've analyzed a progression, visualize how you would play it on your instrument and then perform it. If you transcribed it incorrectly, you'll probably hear the difference between what you're playing and what you heard on the recording right away. This progression includes an inversion (the A/C♯ on beat 2), an example of modal interchange (Dmi, a "borrowed" IV minor chord), and some non-functioning secondary dominants (C7, B7, and B♭7). Despite the apparent theoretical complexity, it's a typical-sounding jazz-blues progression.

The fact is, a fairly small number of chord patterns make up the bulk of the progressions in popular music, with each style favoring certain patterns time and again. As you first begin transcribing, you may need to labor over the scale position and quality of every chord, but over time you can learn to recognize entire patterns of chords (diatonic or not) as familiar sounds.

Melodies Based on Chromatic Progressions

37

By definition, chromatic harmony contains non-diatonic tones, so any melody based on the structure of a chromatic progression would likely include at least some notes outside of the diatonic scale. Again, the number of possible variations is endless, but a basic system for listening and analysis will help you to decipher these melodies.

CD2 Track 26

EXERCISE 1

Listen to **CD2**, **Track 26** and transcribe each melody (with chord progression), following these steps:

1. **Identify the time signature, tonic, and tonality** (major, minor, or dominant). In the first example, the continuous pattern of triplets in the rhythm is best indicated by a compound time signature. Either 6/8 or 12/8 is possible, but since the most common simple time signature in popular music is 4/4, the compound equivalent (12/8) is the best overall choice. The first and last chords are G major, so it's a safe assumption that the key signature is the same.

2. **Identify the chord changes by letter name and quality.** Use the methods you've already learned to identify any non-diatonic chords.

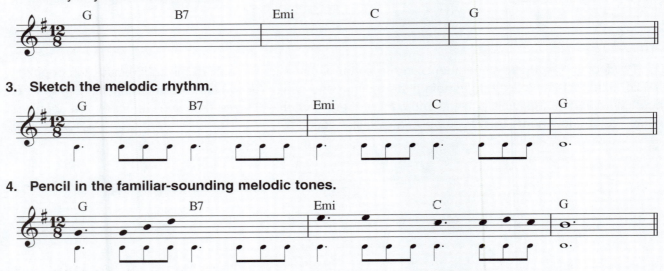

3. **Sketch the melodic rhythm.**

4. **Pencil in the familiar-sounding melodic tones.**

5. **Compare any unusual-sounding notes to the underlying chord or scale.** Sing the arpeggio of the chord and compare it to the melody, listening for matches. Also compare the melody to the underlying diatonic scale, listening for passing or neighboring tones—sometimes this two-directional approach is the best way to confirm the accuracy of the notes. In this example, the B7 chord in measure 1 contains a D♯ (the major third chord degree) that is reflected in the melody. In measure 2, the descending line between Emi and C contains a passing tone, E♭. In each case, the chromatic tone is a half step away from the preceding diatonic tone, so your basic knowledge of whole steps and half steps is again very relevant. Write the rest of the melody on the staff.

6. **Visualize the melody on your instrument.**
7. **Play what you wrote,** and compare it to the original melody.

Modulation
38

Occasionally for the sake of variety, a songwriter decides to change key during a piece of music, a technique called **modulation**. When a tune has modulated, the listener becomes aware that the old tonic no longer applies and a new tonic has taken its place. This shift in tonality may be accomplished through various methods—subtle or abrupt, temporary or permanent—but in any case you must recognize the presence of the new tonic before you can accurately identify the chords and melodies that follow.

Direct vs. Pivot Chord Modulation

Play the following progression on your instrument:

C	F	G	C

C♯	F♯	G♯	C♯

In this progression, the change of key is abrupt—the C♯ (the I chord of the new key) is suddenly and clearly outside the original tonality of C major. From that point on, the tune is in the tonality of C♯; in other words, it has modulated up a half step. This is called a **direct modulation**. As the name implies, direct modulation is a change of key without any preparation. The effect is dramatic and decisive.

Now try this progression:

C	G7	Ami	D7	G	C	D	G

In this example, the modulation is more subtle. The first hint that a new key has arrived occurs when you hear the D7 (the V chord of the new key), but it isn't abrupt as in the first example. Because the A minor chord is common to both keys (C major and G major), it serves to create a smooth transition, easing out of the old key and into the new before you are fully aware that it's happening. When the progression resolves to the new tonic chord, G major, and remains in that key, the modulation is complete. This is called a **pivot chord modulation**—a chord common to both keys (the "pivot chord," in this case Ami) serves as a way of leaving the old key and entering the new one. The effect is smoother than direct modulation, with the actual key change sometimes going unnoticed until after it has occurred.

As in other types of non-diatonic progressions, identifying modulations is sometimes best accomplished by working backward as well as forward. When you hear a new key established and can identify the new tonic chord by comparing it to the original tonic, you can recognize the transitional chords more easily by comparing them to both the old and new keys.

EXERCISE 1

CD2, **Track 27** contains progressions that modulate from the key of C major or minor to other keys, either directly or by pivot chord. Listen to each progression and transcribe the chords, following these steps:

1. Determine the meter and length of the progression. Indicate the tonic (and key signature) at the start.

2. Listen for the key change. You may hear it in the middle of the progression or you may not hear it until the end—mark the place in the progression where you hear the new tonic (I) definitively. Use relative pitch to determine its relationship to the original tonic.

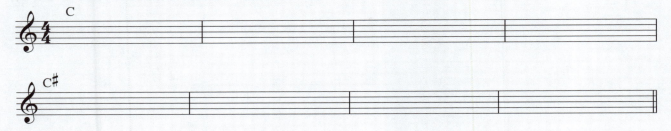

3. Transcribe the letter name and quality of each chord in the progression (singing the bass line, determining chord qualities, etc.) up to the point of modulation.

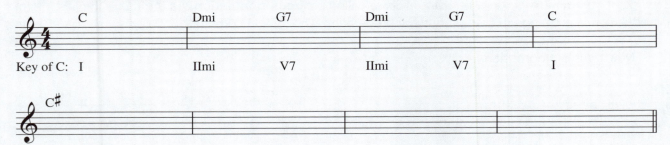

4. At the point of modulation, use the new tonic as your frame of reference to transcribe the remaining chords (working backwards, as needed).

Conclusion

If you've made it to this point from the beginning, you've come a very long way, from learning how to match pitch to hearing practically any melody note over any chord quality with any bass line. But no matter what the particular sounds may be, the most important result of reading this book has been that you've developed a method by which you can hear, understand, and apply the recurring patterns that make up contemporary popular music. Stripping away all of the specific terms and exercises, this method can all be summarized in just a few steps:

- Find "1."
- Identify the rhythm (two, three, or four notes per beat).
- Identify the melody (major, minor, dominant, or chromatic variations).
- Identify the harmony (major, minor, dominant, or chromatic variations).
- Visualize.
- Play.

What's next? In a word, experience. Just as the only way to learn a new language well is to live in a place where it's spoken all the time, to understand music you need to surround yourself with it—listen to it, play it, think about it, and visualize it. Over time, musical patterns that you once had to stop and analyze begin to sound familiar, you can anticipate what the next chord or melody note will be, and you can visualize your fingers playing the patterns. Music is no longer something that exists outside of you—it is part of you. Simply put, that's what great ears are all about.

Answer Key

ach of the exercises contained on the accompanying CDs is transcribed here. Depending on the nature of the exercise, some of the examples are written in number form, and some are in standard musical notation. Refer to the individual chapter and exercise for specific instructions.

Here are a few more tips for getting the most out of the CDs:

- **Listen in a quiet place, free of distractions.** Turn off your telephone. Be aware of background noises; electrical hum, for example, can interfere with your musical perception when you're not aware of it.

- **Work in short (15-30 minute) concentrated sessions.** Short, focused sessions will give you the best results. You don't need to complete each exercise in one sitting—accuracy, not speed, is your priority.

- **Complete each exercise *before* you look at the answer key.** Avoid looking at the key until you've completed the exercise—seeing the answer will distort your ability to evaluate what you can really hear.

- **If at least eight out of ten of your responses match the answer key the first time, move on.** You have a useful understanding of the subject. Return to the exercise only to review mistakes.

- **If your response to any example differs from the answer key, listen to the example again and focus on the differences.** Look for patterns, i.e., certain sounds or combinations of sounds that consistently give you problems. Isolate the difficult area, practice the singing or other exercises that are related to the CD exercise, and then test yourself again.

- **Don't become stuck on any one exercise for too long.** If you go through an exercise several times and still can't reach 80% accuracy, go ahead to the next one. Come back to the problem exercise later. The techniques, ideas, and exercises presented in this book overlap each other, so moving ahead will strengthen skills that you can bring back to the problem exercise. Allowing yourself to become frustrated will not improve your ear.

- **Practice singing, visualization, and playing exercises away from the CDs.** This method is designed around a combination of exercises, not just the CDs alone. Singing and other exercises build your fundamental hearing and analysis skills, and the CDs provide a means to test those skills. Both tools are equally important.

- **If you want more exercises in any given area, create them yourself.** Write and record your own exercises, following the same guidelines used for any particular CD exercise, then listen back and test yourself. As you do this, you'll be strengthening your ear and your understanding of the subject at the same time.

- **Apply your ear training skills to "real" music.** The goal of this method is not to make you better at doing exercises; it's to help you understand the music you like. The exercises help you understand the elements of music, but every style applies those elements in a different way. Your ear training skills will only become usable when you can relate them to the music you already listen to and play.

CD 1

TRACK 1 (Chapter 3, Exercise 4)

*1.	**1**	**2**	**1**	**2**	**3**
2.	1	2	1		
3.	1	2	3		
4.	8	7	8		
5.	1	2	3	4	
6.	1	2	1	2	
7.	1	2	3	2	
8.	8	7	6	5	
9.	1	2	3	2	1
10.	1	2	3	4	5
11.	8	7	6	7	8
12.	1	2	3	4	3
13.	8	7	6	5	4	5
14.	1	2	3	4	5	6
15.	8	7	6	7	6	5

*****boldface** = demonstrated example

TRACK 2 (Chapter 4, Exercise 4)

1.	**1**	**3**	**2**	**7̲**	**1**
2.	1	2	3	1	
3.	1	3	2	1	
4.	1	3	4	5	
5.	8	7	9	8	
6.	1	2	3	5	
7.	8	6	7	8	
8.	1	3	4	2	1
9.	8	7	6	5	3
10.	1	2	7̲	2	1
11.	1	2	4	3	1
12.	8	6	5	7	8
13.	1	3	2	4	5
14.	1	2	3	5	3
15.	1	3	5	6	5
16.	8	7	9	7	8

TRACK 3 (Chapter 5, Exercise 4)

1.	1	5	1		
2.	1	6	1		
3.	1	5̲	1		
4.	8	6	8		
5.	1	3	1		
6.	1	4	1		
7.	8	4	8		
8.	8	3	8		
9.	1	4	3	1	
10.	8	6	5	1	
11.	1	2	3	8	
12.	1	6	5	8	
13.	8	5	4	3	
14.	1	5	7̲	1	
15.	8	3	5	1	
16.	1	5̲	3	1	
17.	1	5	4	3	1
18.	1	2	4	3	8
19.	8	7	6	5	8
20.	1	3	2	5	1
21.	8	5	4	3	1
22.	8	6	5	6	1
23.	1	7̲	2	5	1
24.	1	4	3	2	1
25.	8	3	4	3	1
26.	1	5	6	5	8
27.	8	5	3	5	1
28.	1	3	5	7̲	1
29.	1	2	3	5	1
30.	8	5	6	7	8
31.	1	5	6	7	8
32.	8	10	5	7	8

TRACK 4 (Chapter 5, Exercise 7)

1.	3	2	1		
2.	5	3	1		
3.	3	7̲	1		
4.	7̲	2	1		
5.	7	5	8		
6.	5̲	7̲	1		
7.	3	5	1		
8.	5	7̲	1		
9.	5	3	2	1	
10.	3	4	3	1	
11.	5	6	7	8	
12.	3̲	4̲	5̲	1	
13.	7̲	1	2	1	
14.	3	2	3	1	
15.	7̲	6̲	5̲	1	
16.	5	2	3	1	
17.	5	4	3	2	1
18.	7̲	1	2	3	1
19.	5	8	7	5	8
20.	3	4	3	2	1
21.	7̲	6̲	5̲	7̲	1
22.	3	4	5	3	1
23.	5	6	5	3	1
24.	3	2	1	7̲	1
25.	7	8	6	7	8
26.	5	3	4	2	1
27.	3̲	5̲	6̲	7̲	1
28.	7	5	4	2	1
29.	5	10	8	7	8
30.	3	5̲	1	2	1

TRACK 5 (Chapter 6, Exercise 2)

TRACK 6 (Chapter 6, Exercise 3)

TRACK 7  (Chapter 6, Exercise 4)

TRACK 8 (Chapter 7, Exercise 1)

TRACK 9 (Chapter 9, Exercise 2)

The quality of each second interval is indicated by "ma" for major or "mi" for minor.

1. ma
2. ma
3. mi
4. mi
5. mi
6. mi
7. mi
8. ma
9. ma
10. ma

TRACK 10 (Chapter 10, Exercise 2)

The quality of each third interval is indicated by "ma" for major or "mi" for minor.

1. ma
2. mi
3. ma
4. mi
5. mi
6. ma
7. ma
8. ma
9. mi
10. ma

TRACK 11 (Chapter 10, Exercise 5)

Perfect fourth intervals are indicated by the number "4" and perfect fifth intervals by "5."

1. 5
2. 4
3. 5
4. 4
5. 4
6. 5
7. 5
8. 4
9. 5
10. 4

TRACK 12 (Chapter 10, Exercise 7)

The quality of each sixth interval is indicated by "ma" for major or "mi" for minor.

1. ma
2. mi
3. mi
4. ma
5. ma
6. mi
7. ma
8. mi
9. mi
10. ma

TRACK 13 (Chapter 11, Exercise 2)

The quality of each third interval is indicated by "ma" for major or "mi" or minor.

1. ma
2. mi
3. ma
4. ma
5. mi
6. ma
7. mi
8. mi
9. ma
10. mi

TRACK 14 (Chapter 11, Exercise 4)

Perfect fourth intervals are indicated by the number "4" and perfect fifth intervals by "5."

1. 4
2. 5
3. 4
4. 5
5. 4
6. 4
7. 5
8. 5
9. 5
10. 4

TRACK 15 (Chapter 11, Exercise 6)

The quality of each sixth interval is indicated by "ma" for major or "mi" for minor.

1. ma
2. ma
3. mi
4. ma
5. mi
6. ma
7. mi
8. mi
9. ma
10. mi

TRACK 16 (Chapter 12, Exercise 4)

The quality of each triad is indicated by "ma" for major or "mi" for minor.

1. ma
2. mi
3. ma
4. ma
5. mi
6. mi
7. ma
8. mi
9. ma
10. mi

TRACK 17 (Chapter 13, Exercise 3)

1.	I	VImi	IV	V	I
2.	I	IImi	IIImi	I	
3.	I	V	IV	I	
4.	I	VImi	V	I	
5.	I	IIImi	IV	I	
6.	I	IV	V	I	
7.	I	IImi	V	I	
8.	I	IIImi	V	I	
9.	I	IImi	IV	I	

TRACK 18 (Chapter 14, Exercise 1)

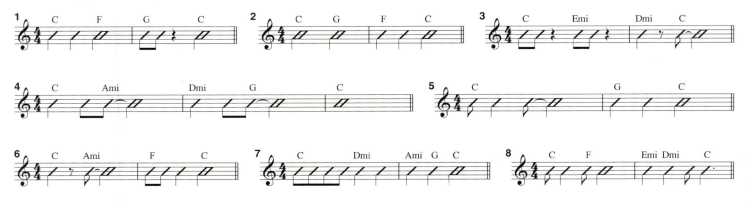

TRACK 19 (Chapter 15, Exercise 3)

TRACK 20 (Chapter 16, Exercise 1)

CD 2

TRACK 1 (Chapter 17, Exercise 4)

Answers indicate scale
degree of note played.

1. ♭3
2. ♭6
3. 2
4. 5
5. 4
6. ♭7
7. 2
8. ♭6

TRACK 2 (Chapter 18, Exercise 1)

1.	1	♭3	1	5	♭6	4	5				
2.	1	2	♭3	♭6	5	♭3	1				
3.	1	2	4	♭3	4	♭6	5	♭7	8		
4.	♭3	2	1	2	♭3	4	5	♭6	4	5	5	1
5.	5	4	♭3	2	1	♭6	5	4	♭3	2	1
6.	1	♭3	1	2	♭3	4	5	♭6	♭7	8	
7.	♭3	2	♭3	1	8	♭7	♭6	5	4	♭6	5
8.	8	5	♭6	5	4	3	2	♭3	4	5	♭3	1

TRACK 2 (Chapter 18, Exercise 2)

TRACK 3 (Chapter 19, Exercise 1)

TRACK 4 (Chapter 19, Exercise 2)

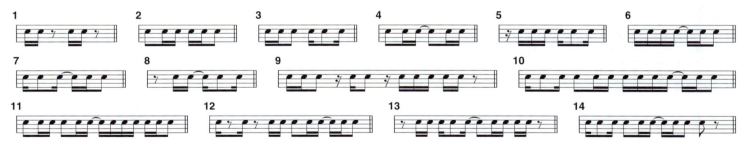

TRACK 5 (Chapter 20, Exercise 1)

TRACK 6 (Chapter 21, Exercise 2)

1. **Imi**   **IVmi**   **♭III**   **♭VII**   **Imi**
2. Imi   ♭VI   Vmi   Imi
3. Imi   Vmi   ♭VII   Imi
4. Imi   IVmi   ♭VI   ♭VII   Imi
5. Imi   ♭III   IVmi   Vmi   Imi
6. Imi   Vmi   ♭VI   IVmi   Imi
7. Imi   ♭VII   ♭III   IVmi   Imi
8. Imi   II°   ♭VI   Vmi   Imi
9. Imi   ♭VII   Vmi   IVmi   Imi

TRACK 7 (Chapter 22, Exercise 1)

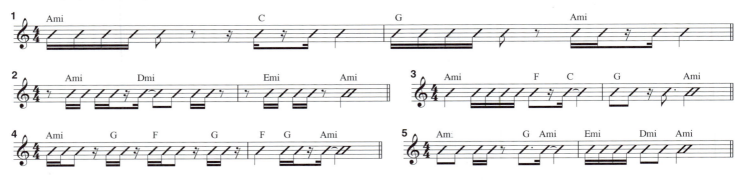

TRACK 8 (Chapter 23, Exercise 1)

TRACK 9 (Chapter 24, Exercise 2)

1. ma7		7. ma7	
2. ma7		8. ma7	
3. mi7		9. mi7	
4. mi7		10. mi7	
5. mi7		11. mi7	
6. ma7		12. ma7	

TRACK 10 (Chapter 24, Exercise 4)

1. major 7		7. dominant 7	
2. dominant 7		8. minor 7	
3. minor 7		9. minor 7 flat 5	
4. minor 7 flat 5		10. dominant 7	
5. major 7		11. minor 7 flat 5	
6. minor 7		12. major 7	

TRACK 11 (Chapter 25, Exercise 2)

1. Ima7   IImi7   IIImi7   Ima7
2. Ima7   IImi7   V7   Ima7
3. Ima7   V7   IVma7   Ima7
4. Ima7   IVma7   IIImi7   Ima7
5. Ima7   IIImi7   VIImi7(♭5)   Ima7
6. Ima7   VImi7   IImi7   V7   Ima7
7. Ima7   VIImi7(♭5)   VImi7   V7   Ima7
8. Ima7   VImi7   IVma7   V7   Ima7
9. Ima7   IVma7   VIImi7(♭5)   IIImi7   Ima7

TRACK 12 (Chapter 25, Exercise 4)

1. Imi7   IVmi7   Vmi7   Imi7
2. Imi7   ♭VIma7   IVmi7   Vmi7   Imi7
3. Imi7   Vmi7   ♭VIma7   Imi7
4. Imi7   IVmi7   ♭IIIma7   Imi7
5. Imi7   ♭VIma7   ♭VII7   Imi7
6. Imi7   IImi7(♭5)   IVmi7   ♭IIIma7   Imi7
7. Imi7   ♭VIma7   IImi7(♭5)   Vmi7   Imi7
8. Imi7   Vmi7   IVmi7   ♭VII7   Imi7
9. Imi7   ♭VIma7   IVmi7   IImi7(♭5)   Imi7

TRACK 13 (Chapter 26, Exercise 4)

TRACK 14 (Chapter 27, Exercise 1)

TRACK 15 (Chapter 28, Exercise 7)

TRACK 16 (Chapter 29, Exercise 2)

TRACK 17 (Chapter 30, Exercise 2)

1.	**I**	**III7**	**VImi**	**V7**	**I**		
2.	I	VImi	II7	V7	I		
3.	I	VI7	IImi	V7	I		
4.	I	I7	IV	V7	I		
5.	I	VII7	IIImi	V7	I		
6.	Imi	♭VII7	♭III	V7	Imi		
7.	Imi	♭III7	♭VI	V7	Imi		
8.	Imi	IV7	♭VII	V7	Imi		
9.	I	III7	VI7	II7	IImi	V7	I
10.	Imi	IV7	♭VII7	♭III7	♭VI	V7	Imi

TRACK 18 (Chapter 31, Exercise 2)

1. Major triad, second inversion
2. Minor triad, second inversion
3. Minor triad, first inversion
4. Major triad, first inversion
5. Major triad, second inversion
6. Minor triad, first inversion
7. Minor triad, second inversion
8. Minor triad, first inversion
9. Minor triad, second inversion
10. Major triad, second inversion

TRACK 19 (Chapter 31, Exercise 4)

1. Dominant seventh, third inversion
2. Dominant seventh, first inversion
3. Major seventh, second inversion
4. Minor seventh, first inversion
5. Major seventh, third inversion
6. Minor seventh, second inversion
7. Minor seventh, third inversion
8. Dominant seventh, second inversion
9. Major seventh, first inversion
10. Dominant seventh, third inversion

TRACKS 18 & 19 (Chapter 31, Exercise 5)

1.	F/C	1.	G7/F
2.	Fmi/C	2.	D7/F♯
3.	Fmi/A♭	3.	B♭ma7/F
4.	E/G♯	4.	Cmi7/E♭
5.	C♯/G♯	5.	Fma7/E
6.	F♯mi/A	6.	Gmi7/D
7.	E♭mi/B♭	7.	Gmi7/F
8.	Emi/G	8.	A7/E
9.	Bmi/F♯	9.	Dma7/F♯
10.	A/E	10.	A♭7/G♭

TRACK 20 (Chapter 31, Exercise 6)

1.	**G**	**D/F♯**	**Emi**	**C**	**D**	**D/F♯**	**G**
	I	**V/3**	**VImi**	**IV**	**V**	**V/3**	**I**
2.	F	B♭/D	C/E	F	B♭	C7	F
	I	IV/3	V/3	I	IV	V7	I
3.	Emi	Bmi/D	Ami/C	Ami	Emi/B	B7	Emi
	Imi	Vmi/♭3	IVmi/♭3	IVmi	Imi/5	V7	Imi
4.	E	E/G♯	A	A/C♯	B/D♯	B	E
	I	I/3	IV	IV/3	V/3	V	I
5.	Cmi	Cmi/B♭	A♭	A♭/G	Fmi	G7	Cmi
	Imi	Imi/♭7	♭VI	♭VI/7	IVmi	V7	Imi
6.	Gmi	Gmi/B♭	Cmi	Gmi/D	Cmi/E♭	Dmi/F	Gmi
	Imi	Imi/♭3	IVmi	Imi/5	IVmi/♭3	Vmi/♭3	Imi
7.	E♭	E♭/G	Fmi/A♭	Cmi/G	Fmi	B♭/D	E♭
	I	I/3	IImi/♭3	VImi/5	IImi	V/3	I
8.	Dmi	C/E	F	Gmi/B♭	Dmi/A	A	Dmi
	Imi	♭VII/3	♭III	IVmi/♭3	Imi/5	V	Imi
9.	D	A/C♯	D/C	G/B	Gmi/B♭	D/A	A7	D
	I	V/3	I/♭7	IV/3	IVmi/♭3	I/5	V7	I

TRACK 21 (Chapter 32, Exercise 4)

1. F6/9
2. B♭6
3. Emi2
4. B5/2
5. Bsus
6. Gmi6
7. F2
8. A♭mi6/9

TRACK 22 (Chapter 33, Exercise 4)

1.	Emi9	6.	B♭ma13
2.	D9sus	7.	A7sus
3.	Dmi11	8.	C9
4.	B♭13	9.	D13
5.	Fma9	10.	C♯mi11

TRACK 26 (Chapter 37, Exercise 1)

TRACK 27 (Chapter 38, Exercise 1)